Stephen Friar
and John Ferguson

Basic
Heraldry

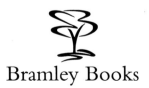

Bramley Books

This edition produced 1999 by A & C Black (Publishers)
Ltd. for Bramley Books, an imprint of Quadrillion
Publishing Ltd.

First edition 1993

ISBN 1-84100-051-5

A CIP catalogue record of this book is available from
the British Library.

Printed in Hong Kong
by South China Printing Company (1988) Ltd

Title page illustration: Device of the Royal Society of St George

Contents

For Barbara

Acknowledgements

The authors acknowledge with thanks the invaluable assistance of members of the Heraldry Society, the Heraldry Society of Canada and the Society of Heraldic Arts in the preparation of this book.

Introduction

Heraldry has rightly been described as 'the shorthand of history' for it relates in symbolic form the hopes and aspirations, the achievements and failures of our ancestors.

Throughout Europe, heraldry is ubiquitous in the architecture and decoration of domestic and ecclesiastical buildings, in illuminated manuscripts and official documents, and on seals, monuments and memorials. But its function is not merely decorative. Heraldic devices were a means of declaiming feudal authority and knightly pre-eminence. They were outward and visible symbols of a man's position and influence, and of his household's status in society. The accumulated quarterings and badges of richly emblazoned memorials proclaimed his ancestry more proudly than any inscription.

The mass emigration of Europeans in recent centuries inevitably resulted in the adoption, in the Americas, southern Africa and Australasia, of European heraldic practices, including those of the English, Irish and Scottish traditions. Heraldry in the Commonwealth is directly related to that of Britain, for its authority is derived from the Crown. In the United States there is no such centralized authority (other than the military Institute of Heraldry), but the European heraldic tradition retains a potent place in the United States' historical perspective and the British heralds continue to devise honorary armorial bearings for those of proven British descent and for corporate bodies. Heraldry also provides a rich source of genealogical and historical information for those who wish to trace their European ancestry.

Stephen Friar and John Ferguson
August 1992

1. Ancient Egyptian provincial vexilloids
2. Typical Roman standard c. 104 BC
3. Aztec military banner
4. Persian shield c. 590
5. Greek citizen soldiers' shields c. 500 BC
6. Viking warrior's shield
7. Shield of the royal bodyguard of King Alfonso III c. 870

I The Origins of Heraldry

It is clear that throughout the Ancient World symbols were used to represent authority and affiliation as they are today. The territorial districts of ancient Egypt, for example, possessed devices by which civil and military authority was recognized, and early Roman standards carried religious and martial symbols such as the eagle, which was later adopted as the device of the Roman legion.

In such well-ordered societies the need for easily recognizable symbols of corporate and military authority is readily apparent, but it is in the pages of the Old Testament that we first find mention of hereditary devices associated with individuals and their extended families:

> Every man of the children of Israel shall pitch by his own standard, with the ensign of [his] father's house … And the children of Israel … pitched by their standards and so they set forward, every one after their families, according to the house of their fathers.
>
> (The Book of Numbers, 2 v.2 and 34)

The Venerable Bede, writing in the early eighth century, describes the banners of King Edwin of East Anglia which 'were not only borne before him in battle, but even in time of peace, when he rode about his cities, towns or provinces … the standard bearer was wont to go before him'. Clearly, these banners bore the symbols of Edwin's dynastic and territorial authority, though Bede does not describe them in detail.

Most of the flags depicted in the Bayeux Tapestry (c. 1077) are of cloth and are small, semicircular or square with a number of 'tails' attached to the fly. That the devices borne on these flags were of territorial or even personal significance has long been a matter of dispute, but it is now generally accepted that the Normans had not, at that time, adopted the proto-heraldic system evident in the lance pennons of their Flemish allies.

It is most likely, therefore, that the origins of British heraldry are to be found, not in Normandy, but in the system adopted by certain ruling families descended from the Emperor Charlemagne who ruled the Frankish Empire of northern Europe from 768 to 814. These families perpetuated much of the administrative organization of the Carolingian Empire, including the use of dynastic and territorial emblems on seals, coinage, customs stamps and flags, indeed 'wherever officialdom needed to identify itself both in peace and war' (Beryl Platts, *The Origins of Heraldry*). There is evidence to suggest that these devices were common to families or groups linked by blood or feudal tenure, and were, of necessity, hereditary. With the redistribution of lands following the Norman Conquest, the cadets in England of Flemish families (who were of Carolingian descent), and the devices used by them, became integrated in Anglo-Norman society.

The traditional theory, that heraldry originated in the decoration of shield and surcoat in order that heavily armoured knights should be identified more easily in battle, is of doubtful validity. Common sense suggests that the mud and debris of warfare would quickly obliterate the battered surfaces of shields, rendering them unrecognizable.

Within the feudal system every man who held land subject to military service was 'known' or 'noted' (in Latin, *nobilis*) and while these obligations were frequently commuted to other services, or to the payment of fines, the feudal *nobilis* retained its clearly defined superiority within a two-tier society in which there was an enormous gap between the upper and lower classes: the 'gentle' and the 'simple'. Armigerous status (in Latin, *armiger* means 'arms-bearer') acknowledged the exclusive right of members of the twelfth-century military élite to possess emblems by which their feudal pre-eminence might be recognized.

The extraordinarily rapid adoption of heraldry throughout western Europe in the early twelfth-century was almost certainly a result of what is now known as the Twelfth Century Renaissance. The exuberance of spirit inspired by this movement expressed itself in a self-confident delight in personal adornment and visual decoration of which the adoption of heraldic symbols and colours was an obvious manifestation. Promoted by the military households (the *familia regis*) of the Angevin kings, popularized by the tournament, communicated throughout Europe by itinerant knights, minstrels and scholars, it was inevitable that the principles of heraldry should eventually be consolidated as an essential element of the law of arms.

Norman cavalry soldier and lance flags from the Bayeux Tapestry

Symbols of Rome and the Ancient Kingdoms

Twelfth-century heraldic devices were very simple and, for the most part, consisted of geometrical figures, stripes and a small number of familiar beasts and birds – sometimes the half-forgotten symbols of Imperial Rome and of the Anglo-Saxon kingdoms.

The dragon standard of the Roman cohort survived in Britain as the 'burning dragon' of Cadwallader, who lived within two centuries of the withdrawal of Rome, and later in the arms attributed by the medieval heralds to the ancestral line of Arthur and Uther Pendragon ('Dragon-head'). These early 'dragons' were two-legged creatures (we would now describe them as *wyverns*), though in post-medieval heraldry the four-legged version is more numerous. A single red dragon in the arms of Somerset County Council recalls Arthurian Glastonbury (Avalon) and Cadbury Castle, and in the civic heraldry of Wales *y ddraig goch* (the red dragon) is ubiquitous, though early chroniclers describe it as being of 'ruddy gold' rather than red.

The golden eagle of the Roman legion is commemorated in the arms of Wallsend at the eastern end of Hadrian's Wall; and the wall itself is represented in stylized form in the gold and red arms of Northumberland County Council. These are a variation of the arms attributed to the ancient kingdom of Bernicia by the medieval heralds, following Bede's description of a 'banner made of gold and purple' which was hung over the tomb of St Oswald, the first Christian king of Northumbria.

It seems likely that the West Saxons usurped the golden dragon in defiance of the native Celts. The famous dragon standard of Wessex, which is said to have been carried by Cuthred at the battle of Burford in 752, by Edmund Ironside at Assingdon in 1016 and Harold on the Senlac ridge in 1066, was probably fashioned from rigid leather and would have been similar in appearance to a gilded weather vane. Several local authorities in present-day 'Wessex' have wyverns in their arms: a twin-tailed and double-headed monster in the crest of Sherborne, Dorset, for example (*see* page 133), and the sea wyvern supporters in the arms of the West Dorset District Council.

The white horse of the Kingdom of Kent, and of the Anglo-Frisian invaders, is recalled in the arms of the Kent County Council and several former boroughs. The names Hengist (of Frisian derivation) and Horsa (Anglian) are synonymous, both meaning 'the Horse', and it seems likely, therefore, that the device was adopted by an Anglo-Frisian chieftain to commemorate his (alleged) descent from the god Odin, one of whose attributes was the magical horse, Sleipner.

Reconstruction of the
Dragon standard of
Wessex

Sea-wyvern supporter from
the arms of West Dorset
District Council

Shields of local authorities:

1. Kent County Council
2. Borough of Wallsend
3. Northumberland
   County Council

The early heralds enjoyed attributing arms to the kingdoms and characters of pre-Conquest Britain.

The six *martlets* attributed to the kingdom of the South Saxons are strange little birds. They have no legs and are said to remain in perpetual and joyful flight and therefore possess all the characteristics of the skylark. They often appear in the civic heraldry of Sussex where they refer, not to the South Saxons or to the skylark, but to the arms adopted by the Norman de Arundel family which are clearly a pun on the word *hirondelle*, meaning swallow.

The arms attributed to Edward the Confessor (1042–66) originated in the silver coins of his reign, which bore a cross between four doves: symbols of piety and gentleness. The arms assigned to the Confessor were *Azure* [blue] *a Cross Flory between five Doves Gold* and references to these may be found in the heraldry of Westminster Abbey, Westminster School, the City of Westminster and Westminster Hospital.

The arms of the (former) county of Middlesex, and those of Essex, contain notched swords or *seaxes* which, it has been claimed, allude to the East Saxons. This tradition is probably attributable to the anonymous continuator of Florence of Worcester's Chronicle who refers to a 'foreign and savage race' whose land was called Saxony after 'these long and victorious knives'. *Seaxes* are to be found in the heraldry of several minor authorities and former boroughs in the southeast of England.

The heralds looked to Scandinavia when devising arms for the kingdom of the East Angles and adopted the arms of Sweden: three gold crowns on a blue background. The martyrdom (in 869) of St Edmund, the last East Anglian King, is commemorated in the arms of Bury St Edmunds, in which each of the crowns is pierced by two arrows. The three crowns on red in the arms of the See of Ely recall its royal foundation by St Ethelreda, while in the arms of Colchester they were combined with two silver *staves raguly* to form a cross, *pierced by Passion Nails*; a reference to the Romano-British tradition that the Empress Helena, daughter of King Coel, discovered the True Cross while on pilgrimage in the Holy Land. In the arms of the (former) Isle of Ely County Council the three crowns are depicted on a red *pile* together with wavy blue and silver lines which represent the fen country. The arms of the University of East Anglia also include three crowns, with a silver *triple-towered castle*, and in the Midlands the emblems of St Edmund the Martyr are to be found in the arms of Oxford University where they reflect the esteem in which he was held by the medieval ecclesiastical establishment. (*See* also page 104)

The Leopards of England

There is little doubt that the 'burning dragon' of Cadwallader, which was usurped by the West Saxons (*see* page 12), was also adopted by William of Normandy even before his conquest of England. Indeed, it is known that 'the terrible standard of the dragon' (Richard of Devizes) was among those used by four of William's successors: Richard I, Henry III, Edward I and Henry V.

It was the thirteenth-century heralds who assigned retrospectively the 'leopards of England' to the Norman kings (in the early language of heraldry all lions of the prowling variety were described as 'leopards'). But it is likely that Henry I (1100–35) was the first English king actually to adopt the lion as a personal device and it was during his reign that the first lion was seen in England – at the royal menagerie at Woodstock. Henry was known as the 'Lion of Justice' and his descendants through his illegitimate children bore one or more lions in a variety of attitudes, and sometimes accompanied by other devices. Where the second lion of England originated remains a mystery, though it has been suggested (not convincingly) that it was acquired through Henry's marriage with Adeliza, the daughter of Godfrey of Louvaine who is also believed to have used a lion device on his seal.

The seal of Eleanor of Aquitaine, wife of the first Angevin king, Henry II (1154–89), bears three lions – indicative, perhaps, of early marshalling (*see* Chapter 8), for Eleanor herself bore a single gold lion on red. Henry's son, John, is known to have borne two lions, and a shield of *three Lions passant guardant* later appears on the second great seal of Richard I (1195) and was used thereafter by succeeding English sovereigns.

Perhaps the best-known Plantagenet device, inherited by Henry II from his father, Geoffrey Plantagenet, Count of Anjou, is the allusive *planta genista*, or broom plant – that which, 'in early summer makes the open country of Anjou and Maine a blaze of living gold'. Plantagenet ancestry was much prized by later English monarchs, and the *planta genista* badge was used by Richard I, John, Henry III, Richard II, Henry IV and even Elizabeth I who had a costume embroidered with broom-pods.

The seal of Eleanor of Aquitaine

Left-hand shield – Norman
Right-hand shield – Plantagenet

Left: The Planta Genista
badge of the Plantagenets

The Crusades

The Wars of the Cross, to free the Holy Land from the infidel, began in 1095 with much optimism and high ideals. They occupied the best of western Christendom's military and religious fervour for three centuries, yet politically they achieved virtually nothing.

Pope Urban II, the preacher of the First Crusade (1095–99), decreed that 'The Cross of Christ is the symbol of your salvation. Wear it, a red, a bloody cross, on your breast and shoulders, as a token that His help will never fail you; as the pledge of a vow which can never be recalled.' During the Third Crusade (1188–92) the red cross was appropriated by the French, to distinguish their forces from those of other countries, a white cross being worn by the English and a green one by the Flemings. But when, in the reign of Edward III (1327–77), the English adopted St George as their patron saint, the red cross became their own and has remained so.

Numerous armigerous families claim that the crosses in their arms are derived from ancestors who fought in the Crusades. But the device is so common in heraldry, and has evolved into so many different forms, that very few who now bear a cross can substantiate their claims (see page 172).

From the Crusades, which coincided with the Twelfth Century Renaissance and the decline of feudalism, emerged a European fellowship of mounted warriors – la chevalerie – bound together by a code of honour and the law of arms. It was, perhaps, inevitable that the concept of knighthood should find expression in the military and religious orders of chivalry of which the Knights Templar and the Knights Hospitaller were pre-eminent examples.

Both the Templars (the Order of the Poor Knights of Christ and of The Temple of Solomon) and the Hospitallers (the Military and Hospitaller Order of St John of Jerusalem) adopted as their badges the eight-pointed cross, each point symbolizing one of the Beatitudes – the qualities of Christian perfection. The Templars also used the Agnus Dei and a strange device, consisting of two knights riding a single horse, which was later misinterpreted and translated into a pegasus in the arms of the Inner Temple, London. The Templars' red cross was worn on the left shoulder of a white habit and their banner, the famous Beau Seant, was divided horizontally, black and white: 'fair and favourable to the friends of Christ, black and terrible to His enemies'. The Hospitallers wore black habits charged with a white eight-pointed cross, and their arms were a plain, white cross on a red field.

Top left: Typical Crusader's pennon *c.* 1200

Top right: Agnus Dei (The Lamb of God) device

Bottom left: Group of mounted Crusader knights from a manuscript in the British Museum

1. The Templars' banner. 2. The badge of the Hospitallers. 3. The Templars' red cross.
4. Early form of the arms of the King of Jerusalem.
5. Later form of the Jerusalem arms.
6. The arms of the Hospitallers

Seals

One of the principal functions of heraldry is to authenticate documents by means of seals which may be found in addition to, or in place of, signatures and are either affixed at the foot of a document or appended to it.

Important documents carried seals before the inception of heraldry in the mid twelfth-century and these often bore distinctive devices which alluded to the names of their owners: a man called Swinford might use a boar (swine) on his seal, for example.

The earliest recorded heraldic seal (that is, one in which the devices are depicted on a shield) dates from 1136 and this, together with a number of seals dating from the mid twelfth century, provides evidence of the rapid spread of heraldry throughout western Europe in a comparatively short period of time. It is also apparent that the use of the same sigillary devices (those found on seals) by succeeding generations of the same family served to consolidate the hereditary nature of heraldry.

Seals are most often found singly but may also represent the parties to a contract. The normal practice in such cases was to prepare a number of copies of a document, each copy (chirograph) being sealed by all the parties to the agreement. The *Constitutions of Clarendon* (1164) were prepared in this way but the three identical documents were never sealed. *Magna Carta* (1215) was sealed by King John's 'five-and-twenty over-kings', and one of the most remarkable medieval documents extant, a letter to the Pope, was signed and sealed (but not delivered) by the ninety-six barons summoned to the Lincoln Parliament of Edward I in 1300. The barons' seals appended to such documents provide some of the earliest contemporary heraldic records in England and the seals themselves demonstrate the diversity of heraldic practice at that time.

In England, the Great Seal of the realm has always been two-sided, like the coinage, with a different device on each side. The first 'great' seal of England was probably that of Edward the Confessor (1042–66) but that which provided a model for later English monarchs was the seal of William I (1066–87) which was engraved on the reverse with the majesty (a depiction of the king seated in state, copied from that of Henri II of France) and on the obverse an equestrian figure, also of the king. Subsequently, the faces were reversed: the majesty becoming the obverse and the equestrian figure the reverse. One of the earliest instances of heraldry in the seal of an English sovereign is to be found in the second seal of Richard I (c.1195) which shows an equestrian figure bearing a shield charged with *three Lions passant guardant* and a fan-shaped crest, also bearing a single lion.

Great Seal of Edward I *c.* 1275

Seal of Thomas de Beauchamp, 1344

Helm and shield of
Richard I from his
second Great Seal

Eustace de Hacche, 1301

John de Warenne, 1301

Gilbert de Pecche, 1301

Simon de Montacute, 1301

Roger de Mortimer, 1301

Kinship

In the early days of heraldry, arms were often modified to signify feudal or blood relationships. Warinus de Strode, for example, as a kinsman of the Duc de Bretagne, bore the arms of Brittany (*Ermine*) to which was added a *Canton Sable* [black] *charged with a Crescent Argent* [silver]; while two members of the Bardolf family bore respectively *Azure* [blue] *three Cinquefoils Gold* and *Azure three Cinquefoils Argent* [silver]. The arms of Luterell (*Gold a Bend between six Martlets Sable*) were used by the de Furnival, d'Eccleshall, de Wadsley, de Wortley and de Mounteney families, each coat 'differenced', by means of a minor variation of colour and design, to signify seigniorial affiliation.

The heraldry in the seals of the twenty-five barons who supervised the execution of *Magna Carta* reflects contemporary feudal and familial kinship. There are five variations of the arms of Clare (*Gold three Chevrons Gules* [red]), including those of Robert FitzWalter, for example, who substituted a red *fess* for the middle *chevron*. Robert de Vere, Earl of Oxford, bore *Quarterly Gules and Gold and in the first quarter a Mullet Argent* [a silver, five-pointed star]. His cousin, John de Lacy, reversed the red and gold quarters and added a narrow black diagonal stripe (*riband*) and a silver *label* to these arms, but omitted the *mullet*; while Geoffrey de Mandeville bore quartered gold and red arms in recognition of his de Vere lineage.

Minor charges were often added to a simple shield in order to distinguish between different members of the same family. To the early Beauchamp arms (*Gules a Fess Gold*) was added a variety of distinguishing charges, including the familiar gold *cross-crosslets* of the Beauchamp earls of Warwick (*see* page 65). The original arms of Cobham (*Gules a Chevron Gold*) were adapted by various members of the family who added, to the *chevron*, three lions, three eagles, three crosses, three *mullets*, three *estoils* [stars], three *fleurs-de-lis* and three *crescents* – all *Sable* [black].

But this was not an invariable practice: the seemingly ubiquitous arms of *three Piles conjoined in base* were used by John le Scot, Earl of Chester (gold with red *piles*) and by the families of Ridel (gold with black *piles*), Basset (gold with red *piles and a Canton Ermine*), de Bryan (gold with blue *piles*) and Wrottesley (gold with green *piles*). In this case only the Wrottesley and Basset families are known to have been related.

FitzWalter

Bardolf

de Mandeville

Luterell

Clare

de Vere

de Lacy

Cobham

de Bryan

Basset

de Strode

Beauchamp

Allusive Arms

Arms often allude to the name, title, office or estate of an armiger and these are correctly termed allusive arms or *armes parlantes*. The punning arms of Sir Thomas Harris of Shropshire, for example, are *Gold three Herrisons* [hedgehogs] *Azure* [blue], and his crest is a golden hedgehog. Hasely, of Suffolk, bore *Argent* [silver] a *Fess Gules* [red] *between three Hazel Nuts Gold* and Cockerell, of London, *Gold a Cross between four Cocks Gules*.

Canting arms are a strict form of allusive arms in which the entire design of a shield is devoted to a pictorial pun on the name or title of the armiger. Instances are numerous in early armory, indeed the frequency of canting arms in the thirteenth and fourteenth centuries suggests that many examples exist which have yet to be identified, the allusion being obscure to the twentieth-century mind. Well-known early examples are those of De Ferres (*Argent six Horseshoes* [ferrs] *Sable*); Trumpington (*Azure two Trumpets pilewise between twelve Cross-crosslets Gold*); and the seven winnowing fans depicted in the brass of Sir Robert de Septvans (d. 1306) at Chartham, Kent. More recently, the arms of Sir Cecil Chubb, first Baronet of Stonehenge, (*Per fess Azure and Vert* [divided horizontally blue and green] *two Pales surmounted by a Chief couped Argent* [silver]) depict a pair of sarsen stones and lintel on a background of sky and grass and allude to Chubb's title, and to his gift of Stonehenge to the nation in 1918. In corporate heraldry, the arms of the British Milk Marketing Board (*Vert* [green] *issuant from the sinister base three Piles wavy bendwise conjoined at the dexter chief point Argent*) are a beautifully simple allusion to the Board's function, as are the arms of the National Coal Board, *Per fess Argent and Sable three Fusils conjoined in fess counterchanged*.

Crests and, of course, mottoes may also be allusive. The arms of the Dymoke family, from 1377 hereditary Champions of England, include a punning motto PRO REGE DIMICO ('I fight for the king') and a crest of two donkey's ears ('deux mokes') which was later changed to those of a hare by disapproving members of the family.

Notable events have also been commemorated heraldically; the *Saracen's Head* crest in the arms of the Lygon, Stapleton, Warburton and Willoughby families recall crusading ancestors, though it should not be assumed that all *Saracen's Head* devices originated in this way and most were adopted several centuries after the event, often replacing an earlier and simpler *panache* (a 'fan' of feathers) or cockscomb crest. The almost identical *moor's head* crests of the Moore and Mordaunt families clearly allude to the names and have no further significance.

Sir Robert de Septvans
1306. After Waller

Harris

Hasely

Cockerell

Chubb

De Ferres

Trumpington

Milk
Marketing Board

National
Coal Board

The Heralds

Clearly, it was considered both convenient and desirable that an heir, on coming to his estate, should adopt the same heraldic device as his father, as a symbol of familial and feudal continuity. Although there is evidence to suggest that, in northern Europe, proto-heraldic devices were often adopted by succeeding generations of the same family (on seals, for example), the emergence of an hereditary system based on the shield (in other words, heraldry as it is now defined) is said to date from 1127 when Henry I of England invested his son-in-law, Geoffrey Plantagenet, with a blue shield charged with gold lions. The same shield later appeared on the tomb (at Salisbury Cathedral) of Geoffrey's bastard grandson, William Longespée, Earl of Salisbury (d. 1226) and the device would therefore seem to have acquired an hereditary significance.

Originally, arms were largely self-assumed by members of the knightly class, though there are examples (including that above) of their being conferred as gifts of feudal superiors or in recognition of military leadership. Arms were (and remain) personal to the armiger and he alone displayed them on his shield and lance pennon and, from the early thirteenth century, on his banner and surcoat (hence a 'gentleman of coat armour' and the term 'coat of arms'). It became necessary, therefore, to ensure that each coat was sufficiently distinctive to avoid confusion with those of men related by blood, by seignioralty or who had simply adopted similar devices from the comparatively small number of figures available at that time. The 'differencing' of arms for this purpose, and the marshalling of two or more coats on one shield to signify marriage alliances, inheritance or the holding of an office to which arms appertained, became an essential (and complex) element of heraldic practice (*see* Chapter 8).

By the beginning of the thirteenth century, admission to the tournament was established as the prerogative of the knightly class. Heralds were attached to royal or magnatial households as advisers and emissaries and it was they who were responsible for arranging tournaments which often lasted for several days and attracted knights from all the countries of western Europe. The heralds thereby acquired an expertise which was peculiarly their own. This was concerned, not only with the management of ceremonial and protocol, but also with the ordering and recording of the personal devices used at tournaments, on seals and in warfare and, because it was they who exercised this expertise, it became known as 'heraldry'.

It was they who enabled heraldry to develop systematically, who devised its conventions and terminology, and who benefited most from the approbation of the medieval Establishment.

Shield of William
Longespée, Earl of
Salisbury

Brass of Sir
Hugh Hastings
showing arms
on surcoat and
shield

Latimer

De Valence

Trussebut

Attributed Arms

The heralds of the medieval and post-medieval periods determined that, because all persons of consequence in their society were armigerous, so too were the characters of their religion and the heroes of legend and history. Just as King Arthur, Charlemagne, Prester John and King David were depicted in medieval costume and leading medieval lives, so were they provided with the heraldic trappings of medieval gentility.

Arms were devised retrospectively, not only for the saints and martyrs, the apostles and disciples and the Old Testament prophets and kings, but also for concepts and abstractions. Banners of the *Scutum Fidei* (the silver and red 'Arms of Faith', symbolizing the Holy Trinity), the *Scutum Salvationis* (the Arms of Salvation) and the Instruments of Christ's Passion accompanied the medieval army into battle, and many a warrior emblazoned the *inside* of his shield with religious emblems.

To the Virgin Mary were attributed several heraldic devices, including a heart, winged in allusion to the angel of the Annunciation and pierced by a sword, on blue shield to signify piety. But while it is the white Madonna Lily (*Lilium Candidum*) which is most readily associated with the Virgin (together with its stylized counterpart, the heraldic *fleur-de-lis*), perhaps the most beautiful device was that of three white lilies in a golden vase, again on a blue field, which was to become a favourite motif of Victorian church restorers.

To the Archangel Michael was attributed a red cross on a silver field and, not to be outdone, Satan himself bore arms (as a former seraph he was assumed to be armigerous): a red shield charged with a gold *fess* (horizontal band) between three frogs, a reference from the Book of Revelation (16 v. 13).

The post-medieval heralds were particularly systematic, beginning with Adam (a plain red shield) and Eve (plain silver). Abel correctly quartered his paternal and maternal arms, though Cain (upon whom God 'set a mark') was required to 'difference' his. To King David the heralds attributed a gold harp on blue and to Joseph, not a multicoloured coat as one might expect, but one of black-and-white chequers.

Equally numerous are arms attributed to legendary characters. To King Arthur were assigned both the arms of St Edmund (*Azure three Crowns Gold*) and *Vert a Cross Argent in the first quarter the Virgin holding the Christ Child Gold*; and to his father, Uther Pendragon, *Gold two Dragons addorsed* [back to back] *crowned Gules* [red]. Merlin bore *Sable semy of Plates* [white roundels on a black field] and to the knights of the Round Table were attributed a variety of arms, the heralds being unable to agree on a definitive list.

PATER NON EST SPIRITUS SANCTUS
NON EST EST EST NON EST
DEUS
EST
FILIUS

Holy Trinity
(Arms of Faith)

The Blessed Virgin Mary

Arms of Christ

Uther Pendragon

The three white lilies
in a golden vase, a
favourite motif of
Victorian restorers

King Arthur

Merlin

Satan

Above: Illuminated letter from a 14C manuscript

Right: 15C tournament parade shield

Below: Figures from an illustrated manuscript, early 14C.

2 The Age of Chivalry

Throughout the Middle Ages, heraldry was considered to be an essential element of the *ius militaris*, the law of arms which, in western and central Europe, prescribed standards of military conduct founded on notions of chivalry and Christian ideals.

Chivalry was both the code of courage and courtesy, which were the ideals of medieval knighthood, and the system of knighthood itself. The terms 'chivalry' and 'cavalry' share the same linguistic root, confirming that knighthood was the prerogative of the mounted warrior. His effectiveness in battle (and, thereby, his reputation) was greatly enhanced by the development, from the eighth century, of the stirrup and saddle-bow which provided both increased manoeuvrability and stability in the saddle.

During the Twelfth Century Renaissance this exclusive class adopted a code of conduct which aspired to the highest ideals though, as history has shown, few of its members succeeded in attaining them. The code comprised three elements:

> Belief in the Church and its defence, especially against the heathen as manifested in the Crusades.
>
> Courage, and loyalty towards a knight's companions, his feudal lord and sovereign.
>
> Respect, pity and generosity in the defence of the weak, the poor and women.

To these were added the notion of romantic love which was to inspire much of the literature of chivalry: Roland in France, Arthur in Britain, El Cid in Spain and the Minnesänger in Germany.

The early chivalric orders were fraternities of like-minded men of the appropriate social class bound together in common purpose: that of the Knights Hospitaller, for example, was to succour pilgrims in the Holy Land. Of course, many members of the early crusading orders were simply adventurers, often the younger sons of knights with little prospect of inheritance and, no doubt, motivated as much by opportunism as by religious or chivalric idealism.

Although modelled on the principles of chivalric egalitarianism and humility, the later medieval orders were essentially élitist, membership being the ultimate reward for loyal service to the sovereign or utilized for the purposes of international diplomacy. Of these, the Most Noble Order of the Garter was pre-eminent (*see* pages 36 and 120).

The Tournament

Tournaments began, in eleventh-century France, as a form of training for battle, later becoming sporting entertainments and, ultimately, occasions of pageantry and ceremonial. Contemporary chronicles described the early tournament as 'a military exercise carried out, not in the spirit of hostility, but solely for practice and the display of prowess.' In the high Middle Ages the tournament became the perfect manifestation of the chivalric ethos.

In the twelfth century the 'aping of the feats of war' consisted of teams of mounted warriors who simply attempted to unhorse one another by force of arms. By the next century, however, the tournament had become more organized and professional jousters travelled throughout Europe seeking and offering challenges. While several (such as the legendary William the Marshal) became very rich, many were killed in combat: the Earl of Salisbury, for example, died of his wounds and his grandson was killed by his own father. In 1292, a *Statute of Arms for Tournaments* required that swords should be blunted and that clubs and maces should not be used. Despite this and other attempts at emasculation, the tournament remained enormously popular. In 1344, for example, the English heralds travelled through France, Brabant, Flanders, Burgundy, Hainault and Scotland publicizing the St George's Day jousts at Windsor and offering safe conduct to the élite of Europe's *chevalerie*.

By that time considerations of good sense generally prevailed: crown-shaped heads replaced the points of lances and special horse harnesses facilitated stability and manoeuvrability and, therefore, safety. The early mixed-weapons free-for-all of the mêlée evolved into a more stylized form known as the tourney in which the two teams of knights fought on horseback according to agreed rules. But the most significant innovation was the stout wooden barrier which separated opponents in what became known as the tilt and the barriers. In the tilt, individual knights, locked in harness and heavily armoured, would attempt to unhorse one another with blunted lances while charging along the barrier; while participants in the barriers fought on foot, with sword or pike, across the wooden barrier.

The heralds organized all the tournament activities, recording the devices borne by participants and keeping scores on jousting cheques.

By the sixteenth century the joust had become 'the ceremonial shattering of fragile, deeply grooved lances, and the literary and pageant elements already dominant in its history gained almost complete ascendancy' (R. C. Strong). Nevertheless, the death of Henri II of France in 1559, who was killed by the splintered lance of Gabriel de Montgomerie, failed to dampen the enthusiasm for tournaments among the nobility and they continued, as bloodless spectacles, well beyond the Elizabethan period.

14c Tournament pavilion

Jousting knights. From the *Manessa Codex*

The arms of William
the Marshall

Coronals, the jousting lance heads

Participation, both in the tournament itself and in the attendant festivities, was restricted to those of knightly rank and was enormously expensive. Indeed, throughout the Middle Ages, the cost of maintaining a horse and equipment was such that membership of the warrior élite presupposed a man of some position and estate. It is also clear that the use of hereditary devices on shields was considered to be the exclusive right of this knightly class. Pride in the status of armiger that such a privilege implied, and its manifestation in the richly emblazoned trappings of the tournament, was undoubtedly of greater significance in the development of heraldry than was its application in the field of battle. The heraldic exuberance of the medieval knight is evident in contemporary illustrations, notably that of Sir Geoffrey Luterell in the fourteenth-century Luterell Psalter. The Luterell arms, *Azure* [blue] *a Bend between six Martlets Argent* [silver], are repeated no fewer than nineteen times in Sir Geoffrey's shield, crest, surcoat, pennon and ailettes (shoulder guards); on his horse's caparison, chanfron (head guard), headpiece and saddle bow; and in the gowns worn by his wife and daughter-in-law.

Of all the elements of the coat of arms, that most closely associated with the tournament is the crested helm. While the shield was the symbol of the armiger, the crest was that of knightly superiority. Twelfth- and thirteenth-century crests were simple fan-shaped extensions of the helmet, known as 'cock's combs', on which were painted devices similar to those on the shield (*see* page 21). Panaches ('fans') of feathers were also popular and these may have originated in the built-up spines of Greek and Roman helmets which strengthened the vulnerable area at the back of the head but were also embellished for decorative purposes and to signify rank.

The ornate, modelled crests of the late-medieval tournament were far removed from the simple cock's comb and panache. They were made of light materials (paste board, cloth or boiled leather over a wire frame or basketwork) and were fastened to the helm by laces or rivets, the unsightly join concealed by a coronet or wreath of twisted silk, or by the material of the crest itself, the lower edge of which formed the mantling, often in the form of a beast's fur or feathers.

Many tournament crests originated in personal devices (notably beasts and chimerical creatures) which had been used by succeeding generations (as badges and in the interstices of seals, for example) and which were later translated into heraldic supporters. Inherited coats could be marshalled together in a single shield, but only one crest could be worn. An armiger would therefore select the most prestigious of his inherited crests for this purpose.

Swan's head crest,
probably made of
boiled leather over a
framework of wire

Fan crest of
Sir Geoffrey Luterell

Varied examples of 14C crests
depicted on stall plates of
Garter knights in St George's
Chapel, Windsor Castle

The Order of the Garter

The twin strands of the Arthurian chivalric tradition and the exclusive nature of the tournament are evident in the foundation of the Most Noble Order of the Garter, though even today there exists some doubt as to precisely when this was – for the original records of the Order, up to the year 1416, are lost.

Edward III and his court rejoiced in the chivalric ethos of the Arthurian legends. Pageants (called 'Round Tables') included tournaments at which two teams, each of twelve knights, fought under the leadership of the king and his eldest son, and these were followed by feasting at a circular table. It is likely that from these festivities evolved the notion of a brotherhood of young men, a fellowship in which all were equal, 'to represent how they ought to be united in all Chances and various turns of Fortune, co-partners in both Peace and War, assistant to one another in all serious and dangerous Exploits and through the whole Course of their Lives to show Fidelity and Friendliness towards one another'.

The informal creation of the Round Table after the great tournament at Windsor in 1344 was translated, probably on St George's Day 1348, into the Order of the Garter – twenty-four young men together with the king and his eldest son, Edward Plantagenet, the Black Prince. The Treasury accounts for November 1348 record the gift of '24 garters to the knights of the Society of the Garter'. These were the founder knights 'foreshadowing a distinguished line of noble successors throughout the history of English chivalry'.

The symbol of the blue garter is traditionally said to have been suggested by an incident at a ball at Calais in the autumn of 1347 when the young Countess of Salisbury, Joan of Kent (later to be Princess of Wales) dropped her garter, which the king retrieved and tied below his knee with the now famous words, *Honi soit qui mal y pense* – 'Shame on him who thinks evil of it' – and a promise that the garter would become highly honoured. There may be an element of truth in this, but the garter was not an exclusively female accoutrement (there are numerous contemporary illustrations of its use by men) and it seems likely that it was adopted because of its suitability both as a device (in stylized form) and for its prominence when worn below the knee of a mounted knight.

Although modelled on the principles of chivalric egalitarianism and humility, the Order of the Garter was essentially élitist, membership being the ultimate reward for loyal service to the sovereign or utilized for the purposes of international diplomacy.

The earliest surviving Garter stall plate, that of Ralph, Lord Basset, probably dating from his death in 1390. St George's Chapel, Windsor

Embroidered mantle badge c. 1855. Worn upon the upper left side of the Garter mantle

Sir Nele Loryng KG, wearing the original form of Garter robe, c. 1400. Redrawn from an early manuscript

The Lion and the Fleur-de-Lis

Alexander III of Scotland (reigned 1249–86) is known to have used a *Lion rampant Gules* [red] on a gold field, and it is likely that the device was inherited from his grandfather, William, who was known as 'the Lion'. There is a tradition that the red *double tressure flory* [a double border ornamented with fleurs-de-lis] was added to the royal arms of Scotland to signify an ancient alliance with France whose sovereigns bore *Azure* [blue] *semy-de-lis Argent* [scattered with silver *fleurs-de-lis*]. The *Tressure of Scotland* is found in the arms of several families, many of whom are descended from the royal house or were granted augmentations to their arms in recognition of service to the Scottish Crown (*see* page 103).

The heraldic fleur-de-lis is a stylized lily, probably the Madonna Lily (*Lilium Candidum*) and, as a symbol of purity, is generally associated with the Blessed Virgin Mary. It is the emblem of French sovereignty – 'the Flower of Louis' – and was first borne by Louis VII (1137–80) on a royal seal.

When, in 1337, Edward III of England laid claim to the French throne, declaring himself *Rex Angliae et Franciae*, he quartered the royal arms of France (in the first and fourth quarters – as the senior kingdom in the medieval hierarchy) with those of England. By this time, the royal arms also included a crest: *a Lion statant guardant crowned Gold* on a red chapeau [cap], lined with ermine. Clearly, the *statant* [standing] position of the beast (those in the shield of arms are *passant* [walking]) enabled the modelled crest to be affixed more conveniently to a helmet. Similarly, the *guardant* [looking outwards] position of the beast's head is an heraldic solecism, for on a real helmet (such as the Black Prince's helm at Canterbury Cathedral) the crest would be modelled with the head in the 'forward' position (*see* page 41).

In 1376, Charles V of France reduced the number of *fleurs-de-lis* in his arms to three and, when a new great seal was struck for Henry IV of England in 1405, it too bore the new French arms in the first and fourth quarters – arms which became known as 'France Modern' to distinguish them from the earlier (and infinitely more attractive) 'France Ancient'. Why Charles V chose to alter his arms remains a mystery, though it has been suggested that he did so in order to commemorate the fifth-century Queen Clothilde who presented her husband, King Clovis, with a gift of a holy cloth, embroidered with three lilies.

These arms continued in use until 1603, when James VI of Scotland succeeded Elizabeth I as James I of England, the fleurs-de-lis of France remaining in the royal arms of British sovereigns until 1801.

1337 ~ 1405

1405 ~ 1603

The Prince of Wales

Edward III and his eldest son, Edward, Prince of Wales, were 'Renownèd for their deeds as far from home / For Christian service and true chivalry' (Shakespeare). The foundation of the Order of the Garter in 1348 and the military prowess of his son, 'that young and princely gentleman', confirmed Plantagenet pre-eminence in Europe's chivalric élite.

The ostrich feather badge adopted by the younger Edward (and by several of his brothers and their descendants), may have originated in a similar device used by the family of his mother, Philippa of Hainault, in punning allusion to the county of Ostrevans which was held by the eldest sons of the Counts of Hainault. The Prince's arms were, of course, the quartered *fleurs-de-lis* and leopards of the English sovereign, with the addition of the silver *label* of an eldest son. But on festive occasions, such as tournaments, he used a black shield charged with three silver ostrich feather badges – described as his 'Shield for Peace' – together with the motto ICH DIENE which was either a corruption of the Welsh *Eich Dyn*, meaning 'Your Man', or was of German derivation, meaning 'I serve'. Certain of the Prince's armed retinues may also have worn black livery and it was the brutal zeal of his soldiery during the French *chevauchées* of 1355–6 that acquired for Edward his ruthless reputation and the soubriquet 'Black Prince'.

The term 'Prince of Wales Feathers' is erroneously used to describe the badge of the heir apparent to the English throne. It is clearly derived from the Black Prince's device and comprises three white ostrich feathers enfiling a gold coronet and, on a blue scroll, the motto ICH DIEN. The badge of the Prince of Wales is *y ddraig goch*, the red dragon, depicted on a green mount and with a white *label* of three points about its neck. The arms of the Principality, attributed by the medieval heralds to the native princes of Wales, are *Quarterly Gold and Gules* [red] *four Lions passant guardant counterchanged*, and these are now borne by the Prince of Wales on a small shield (inescutcheon) which is placed upon his arms as heir apparent. As Duke of Cornwall he uses the arms *Sable* [black] *fifteen Bezants* [gold discs] and the motto HOUMOUT, meaning 'magnanimous', which was also used by the Black Prince. The future Edward I was created Earl of Chester in 1245 and since that time (with the exception of a short period when the earldom was held by Simon de Montfort) the dignity has been held by the heirs apparent to the Crown, together with the arms *Azure* [blue] *three Garbs* [wheatsheaves] *Gold*, though these are rarely depicted.

houmout

ich diene

Shield for War

Shield for Peace

ICH DIEN

Badge of the Heir Apparent

Badge of the Prince of Wales

Principality of Wales

The Black Prince's
crested iron helm

Duchy of Cornwall

The Hundred Years War

It was during the Hundred Years War (1337–1453) that the *ius militaris*, the law of arms, reached its apotheosis. Deeds of valour and signal service were commemorated heraldically by the granting of 'honourable augmentations' or, in some cases, by substituting new arms for old. The best-known example is that of John Codrington, banner-bearer to Henry V 'in battaile, watch and ward', who bore as arms a red *fess* [a broad horizontal band] between three red lions, all on silver. His service 'to the worship of knighthood' was commemorated in a grant to his descendants which changed his red *fess* to *Sable fretty Gules* [black with a red trellis-like pattern] – an augmentation that was bound to attract attention for it deliberately flouted the basic convention of heraldry (*see* page 150). A further example, from Agincourt, is the augmentation granted for bravery to John de Wodehouse who changed his *Chevron Ermine* to a *Chevron Or goutty de sang* – gilded and scattered with drops of blood. Many men received heraldic honours of their superiors. Sir James Audley, who fought at Poitiers and whose arms were *Gules fretty Gold*, granted augmentations to a number of his esquires including John de Delves who added a *Chevron Gules fretty Gold* to his punning arms of *Argent* [silver] three *Delves Sable* [three black billets].

Crests were also augmented: to the Walnut Tree of Waller, for example, was added the shield of Charles, Duke of Orleans whom Waller captured at Agincourt. Other devices, commemorative of the French wars, were often incorporated retrospectively. Sir John Pelham, one of several knights and esquires to have claimed responsibility for the capture of the French King, John, adopted as a badge the King's sword buckle, two of which were later quartered on red together with the Pelham arms of three silver pelicans on blue.

Military commanders were accompanied in the field by their banner-bearers and it was considered a disgrace to lose one's banner in battle. Both the banner-bearer and the flag were termed 'lieutenant', while the standard (*see* page 60) was known as the 'ancient', as was the officer who maintained it: hence 'The lieutenant is to be saved before the ancient' (Shakespeare). Military command was the prerogative of the nobility – including the bannerets, lesser barons whose rank was between that of baron and knight bachelor. Knights, who led their own retinues but rarely exercised command, carried triangular or swallow-tailed pennons which, like banners, were emblazoned with their personal arms. Unanticipated promotion in the field of battle to the rank of banneret could be signified by the removal of the pennon's tails to form a small banner (a banneret): Sir John Chandos (1367) and Sir Thomas Trivett (1380) were promoted in this way (*see* page 60).

1. **a.** Arms of John Codrington
   b. Augmented version
2. **a.** Arms of John de Wodehouse
   b. Augmented version
3. **a.** Arms of John de Delves
   b. Augmented version
4. 'Docked' pennons of Sir Thomas
   Trivett and Sir John Chandos

The Cinque Ports

Following the naval victory over the French at Sluys in 1340, Edward III's reputation as 'Lord of the Sea' was reflected in his coinage: 'Four things our noble sheweth to me / King, Ship and Sword, and power of the Sea.' The design of Edward's gold noble is similar to the arms of Dartmouth, a port which furnished ships for the French wars: *Gules* [red] *on Water in base proper an Ancient Ship issuant from the centre thereof the Figure of a King robed crowned and holding a Sceptre and on the Bow and Stern of the Ship a Lion sejant guardant all Gold.*

The Cinque Ports, a federation of ports in the south of England, were the mainstay of England's medieval navy – though by the fourteenth century their influence was already in decline. Dover, Hastings, Hythe, Romney and Sandwich (and, later, Rye and Winchelsea) enjoyed immunities from taxation and military service in return for providing naval defence, an arrangement that is known to have existed long before they received their charters of incorporation from Edward I.

The ancient arms of the corporation were three golden ship's hulls on a blue field but these were later combined with the leopards of England, using an early device called dimidiation (*see* page 181), to produce a strange shield in which the leopards appear to have hind quarters composed of ships' sterns. Sandwich, Winchelsea and Rye continue to use these arms, though only the first does so with any authority and the colour of the ships' hulls is changed from gold to silver. Hastings removed the central hull leaving a lion with its hind quarters intact, while St Martin in the arms of Dover is surrounded by a *Bordure of England* [a red border charged with gold lions]. Hythe and Romney (which once bore three gold lions on blue) no longer have arms but, within the organization of the Cinque Ports, the port of Deal was attached to Sandwich and uses a modified version of the Sandwich arms. Similarly, Faversham was associated with the Cinque Ports and this is reflected in its (unofficial) arms: *Gules three Lions passant guardant parted palewise* [divided vertically] *Gold and Argent.* The arms of Margate and Ramsgate, as associates of Dover and Sandwich respectively, both include *a demi Lion passant guardant joined with the stern end of a Ship's Hull*; and in the arms of Tenterden, a former member of the port of Rye, a ship's mainsail is charged with the arms of the Cinque Ports, though the ships' hulls are silver.

Great Yarmouth in Norfolk contributed more to Edward III's wars than any other port. The town's ancient herring fair was controlled by the Cinque Ports and the original arms of three gold herrings on a blue field are dimidiated with leopards – to strange effect.

1. English gold noble. Edward III
2. Arms of Dover
3. Arms of Sandwich
4. Arms of Hastings
5. Arms of New Romney
6. Arms of Great Yarmouth
7. Common seal of Hythe. Late 13c

Guilds and Livery Companies

Guilds originated in the twelfth century as religious fraternities which evolved round a church, monastery or hospice to which they attached themselves and whose saint they adopted as their patron. Members of those fraternities who lived together often shared in a common trade or craft. They made provision for the poor, sick and needy of their communities and promoted the interests of their 'mystery' or craft, granting apprenticeships and exercising the power of search which gave each company the right to inspect all goods handled by its members. This provided the guilds with an effective weapon against competition and enabled them to maintain high standards of work so that membership became a privilege. A guild's authority was obtained through royal charter and since 1560 their successors, the livery companies, have also been required to apply for a grant of livery from the Court of Aldermen who have to be satisfied that 'a number of men of good repute from some trade or mystery not already represented by an existing guild have joined together for a time sufficiently long to justify the belief that they will continue to hold together and are not likely to fall apart from lack of interest or support'. A liveryman is both a freeman of his city and a senior freeman of his guild who is entitled to wear the uniform (livery) of his company and to exercise other privileges. In due course, by seniority, he becomes eligible for membership of a guild's governing body (Court of Assistants) and thereafter may advance through the various degrees of Warden and Master.

Evidence of the religious origins of the earliest guilds may be found in the arms granted to a number of companies during the second half of the fifteenth century. Those of the Mercers, for example, which depict the Virgin Mary within a border of clouds; and the head of St John the Baptist in the crest of the Tallow Chandlers – an allusion to the company's foundation as the religious fraternity of St John.

Many words and phrases in common usage originated in the livery companies: 'on tenterhooks' from the double-ended hooks in the Clothworkers' arms; 'baker's dozen' in the Bakers' provision of the vantage loaf to avoid incurring a fine for short measure. 'At sixes and sevens' originated in the struggle of the Merchant Taylors and the Skinners companies for sixth and seventh places in the table of precedence; 'hallmarking' from the marking of precious metals at Goldsmiths Hall in London; and, at the completion of his apprenticeship, the submission by an aspiring smith of his first piece of craftsmanship – his 'masterpiece' – to the Master and Wardens of the Company of Goldsmiths.

1

2

3

4

Crest of the Tallow Chandlers 1602

HONOR DEO

The arms of
The Worshipful Company of Mercers

5

6

7

8

The shields:

1. Merchant Taylors. 2. Glovers.
3. Fletchers. 4. Cutlers. 5. Salters.
6. Haberdashers. 7. Skinners.
8. Vintners

Medieval Seals

Medieval seals were usually circular in shape, pointed ovals being used by ecclesiastics – though not exclusively so – and the more important seals were usually impressed on both sides and appended to documents by means of cords.

The Great Seal is still used to authenticate important documents issued in the name of the sovereign and the matrix is held by the Lord Chancellor who was sometimes also referred to as the Lord Keeper (of the Seal). Holders of offices of state, and of the Royal Household (such as the Kings of Arms), use the seals of their office to authenticate official documents, and when an individual holds several offices he uses a separate seal for each.

The *privatum sigillum* or privy seal was, in England, a twelfth-century innovation and was held by the clerks of the King's Chamber. It was used to authenticate warrants by which documents would be issued under the Great Seal, particularly instructions to the Exchequer or Chancery. It was also appended to lesser documents which nevertheless required royal approval. By the fourteenth century the authority of the Privy Seal rivalled that of the Great Seal and in the reign of Edward II (1307–27) a *secretum* was introduced for the sovereign's personal use (Latin *secretum* = 'something hidden').

Inevitably, from the early thirteenth century, it became fashionable for the lords also to engrave their seals with equestrian figures of themselves in armour, complete with heraldic shields, horse-cloths (caparisons) and banners. These seals were often so large, and documents so numerous, that privy seals were required for administrative purposes. These were smaller and, therefore, less ornate than great seals and usually bore a simple shield within a decorative interstice and legend. A *secretum*, perhaps a signet ring, was generally used for private matters and, because of their small size, these often bore devices other than coats of arms: the bear and ragged staff badges of Richard Nevill (d. 1471), for example.

Whereas a simple shield was ideally suited to a circular seal, the elongated fourteenth-century coat of arms, with its helm and crest, created awkward spaces between the central motif and the surrounding legend. These were filled with architectural and decorative patterns (diaper) together with heraldic devices and the figures of beasts or chimerical creatures. These were often personal or household badges which, from the fifteenth century, were frequently translated into crests and supporters (*see* page 85).

Several seals depict stylized sailing ships: that of John, Earl of Huntingdon, Admiral of England (1436), for example, in which the arms *England with a Bordure of France* cover the entire sail.

1. Seal of John, Earl of
   Huntingdon and Admiral
   of England, 1436

2. Seal of Henry, Earl of
   Lancaster and Leicester, 1301

3. Signet ring of Richard
   Nevill 'the Kingmaker', 1471

4. Seal and counter seal
   of Henry de Percy, 1301

5. Ecclesiastical seal
   of Pascal, Abbot of St Mary
   of the Graces, London, 1420

Rolls of Arms

A roll of arms is any collection of heraldry, whether painted, tricked (drawn in outline with colours indicated by abbreviations) or listed in written form using blazon (the language of armory).

The term is most often applied to strips of vellum or parchment, sewn together in rolls or bound into books, on which series of shields or heraldic figures have been painted or tricked. Many of these manuscripts are of medieval origin, though most surviving rolls are later copies and compilations. Rolls of arms illustrate not only the development of the terminology and conventions of heraldry but also the variety and exuberance of artistic interpretation.

The study of rolls of arms dates from the thirteenth century when heralds and chroniclers exchanged information concerning heraldic devices and compiled their own reference works (armorials) and commentaries. In their simplest form, rolls of arms are little more than hastily illustrated lists which were compiled 'on the spot' – at a tournament, for example. Others, such as the Rous and Salisbury rolls, are magnificent pictorial records of the great magnatial families or of significant historical events.

There are some 350 surviving European medieval rolls of arms, of which 130 are English. These are usually classified as Occasional Rolls, which relate to events such as expeditions, tournaments or sieges; Institutional Rolls, associated with foundations and religious and chivalric orders; Regional Rolls, which list the arms of armigers in a particular administrative area such as a county; Illustrative Rolls which illustrate stories or chronicles and may therefore contain attributed arms such as those of the Knights of the Round Table; and General Rolls which are combinations of other types.

The earliest known roll of arms is that of the thirteenth-century monk and historian Matthew Paris whose *Liber Additamentorum* (c. 1244) includes painted sheets illustrating shields of arms. Some rolls of arms contained paintings of historical characters, together with their armorial devices. The Rous or Warwick Roll, for example, is a vellum manuscript, 28 cm wide (11 inches) and 7.5 metres in length (25 feet), in which each of the sixty-three principal characters is described in detail. The roll was compiled between the years 1477 and 1485 by John Rous, a chantry priest and antiquary, as a chronicle of the Earls of Warwick, and the accompanying drawings provide a wealth of heraldic information. The first version, in English, included a laudatory passage to Richard III but, following the accession of Henry VII, this was replaced, in a second Latin version, by a vilification of his former king.

Above: The King of Arms of the Duke of Brittany presenting a tournament roll. From a manuscript painted *c.* 1460

Right: Part of the 15C *Dering Roll*. A copy of an original 13C. roll of mostly Sussex and Kentish families

Below: Two 'tricked' shields from *Some Feudal Coats of Arms* by Joseph Foster, a work compiled from heraldic rolls dating from 1298 to 1418

One of the most important heraldic documents to have survived is the *Armorial de Gelre*, a magnificent roll of arms compiled between 1370 and 1395 by Claes Heijnen, Gelre Herald to John de Blois. This contains 1,687 coats of arms of the leading armigerous families of Europe, to which a further seventy-five were added in the fifteenth century.

The *Armorial Equestre de Toison d'Or*, an early fifteenth-century roll of arms compiled by Jean le Fèvre, King of Arms to the Order of the Golden Fleece, contains a series of brilliantly coloured and animated paintings of the knights of the Order, depicted on horseback with gloriously emblazoned crests, tabards and caparisons. It has rightly been described as 'the quintessence of heraldic vigour and vivacity'.

An ordinary of arms is an heraldic work of reference which lists the descriptions (blazons) of shields alphabetically by the charges they contain. The first ordinary of arms is referred to as 'Cooke's Ordinary' after Robert Cooke, Clarenceux King of Arms, who owned it in 1576. It is a roll of arms, dated *c.* 1340, and is arranged by reference to armorial charges: shields with crosses, those with lions, eagles and so on. The original is owned by Sir Anthony Wagner but there is a tricked sixteenth-century copy by Robert Glover (Somerset Herald 1570–88) at Queen's College, Oxford and this includes also the Baliol Roll of *c.* 1332 which is the earliest known role of Scottish arms.

The Heralds' Visitations of the sixteenth and seventeenth centuries produced numerous records of pedigrees and painted or tricked sketches of arms which were later transferred to the manuscript volumes which now comprise the Library of Visitation Books at the College of Arms and remain the only definitive record (*see* page 86). These may be regarded as regional rolls and, being concerned with the aspirations and self-perceptions of society within the counties and hundreds of England at that time, they provide a fascinating and invaluable source of information.

By the sixteenth and seventeenth centuries many 'editions' of earlier medieval rolls of arms were known and to these were added further listings, compiled by heralds and antiquaries, of collections derived from the Wars of the Roses, the Tudor progresses and heralds' visitations. Notable among these antiquaries was a group led by William Dugdale who, fearful of the 'impending conflict' in the early seventeenth century, began transcribing rolls of arms dating from the mid thirteenth century onwards. The resulting, remarkable collection of painted copies is now at the Society of Antiquaries in London.

1. William Beauchamp, Earl of Warwick. Drawing developed from the original illustration in the *Rous Roll*, *c.* 1480

2. The Duke of Brieg, from the magnificent *Armorial Equestre de Toison d'Or*, compiled by Jean le Fevre in the early 15C

3. The arms of Sir William Dugdale, Garter King of Arms, 1677

1. The Lion of March supporting the livery banner of Edward IV featuring the white rose en soleil. From a design in *Prince Arthur's Book*, 1502

2. Arms of the West Riding of Yorkshire. Granted 1927

3. Badge of Lancaster Herald of Arms in Ordinary

4. Badge of York Herald of Arms in Ordinary

5. Mounted page from the *Westminster Tournament Roll* 1511

3　The Wars of the Roses

'I prophesy: this brawl today …
Shall send between the red rose and the white,
A thousand souls to death and deadly night.'

The popular notion that the houses of York and Lancaster adopted their respective white and red roses in the Temple garden belongs entirely to Shakespeare (*Henry VI Part 1*, Scene 4) while the term 'Wars of the Roses' may be attributed to Sir Walter Scott's *Anne of Geierstein* which he wrote in 1892.

According to Shakespeare, Somerset and Plantagenet invited the assembled company to pluck red or white roses from the bushes in the Temple garden on the understanding that he who received the lesser support should 'yield the other in the right opinion'. In the event, three white roses were picked but only one red. 'Now, Somerset, where is your argument?' challenged Plantagenet. 'Here, in my scabbard, meditating that / Shall dye your white rose to a bloody red' replied 'proud Somerset'.

Shakespeare's knowledge of heraldry was considerable and there can be little doubt that he was aware that the red and white rose badges were in use long before this famous (and probably fictitious) quarrel took place.

The golden rose had been a royal badge since its introduction into English heraldry by Henry III's queen, Eleanor of Provence, and was used by all three Edwards, the Black Prince and Richard II. Its 'cousin', the red rose, had been associated with the title of Lancaster since its adoption by Eleanor's second son, Edmund 'Crouchback', and descended to John of Gaunt through his marriage with the Lancastrian heiress, Blanche. It thereby became the device of the Lancastrian kings and of Gaunt's illegitimate Beaufort line, notably John Beaufort, Duke of Somerset.

A white rose was a badge of Roger Mortimer, second earl of March (d. 1360), grandfather of Richard II's heir, also Roger, fourth earl of March (d. 1398). It was by his Mortimer descent that Richard Plantagenet, Duke of York, laid claim to the throne of England and it seems likely that he selected the white rose from among his many badges to emphasize his aspirations.

Livery and Maintenance

Livery and maintenance, the practice of maintaining and protecting large numbers of retainers in return for administrative and military services, was common throughout Europe during the fourteenth and fifteenth centuries, when a magnate's influence was judged by the number of men wearing his badge and liveries and his ability to protect them when necessary in the courts of law. Some retinues were little better than brigands, terrorizing their lord's neighbours, seizing lands and bearing false witness against them in law suits, while others included the younger sons of the nobility, men of knightly and gentle rank and clerics who often possessed considerable administrative and scholastic ability.

In England, the successful governance of the kingdom came to depend on the system which is now known as 'bastard feudalism'. Parliament met only occasionally, and when not in session the sovereign needed to secure the co-operation of the medieval establishment through whom he ruled. This was achieved through the appointment of the lords and gentry to public office and through an informal system which relied on voluntary service and a sense of obligation to a superior – often referred to as 'worship' in contemporary documents. The sovereign's principal subjects thereby enjoyed considerable political autonomy. Their power rested, not on lineage, but on the acquisition of wealth and influence, and was reflected in the number and quality of the men at their command. They created retinues of indentured servants, and others whose support was based on patronage, who were employed to manage a lord's estates, to hold public office on his behalf and to settle his legal affairs. In time of war, or in defence of their superior, these men were summoned to array. Indeed, many of the more senior members of magnatial households were themselves men of substance, capable of raising significant numbers of indentured retainers in their own right. Provincial political life revolved around these affinities and a magnate was expected to satisfy the aspirations of his followers. When he succeeded, his reputation was enhanced and he thereby attracted more and better men to his service. Royal favour, and the ability to bestow offices, pensions and promotions on his followers, was therefore essential to the expansion of a lord's influence.

The ability of a magnate to summon to the field of battle large retinues of men whose allegiance was secured through the practice of livery and maintenance was a characteristic of the late Middle Ages – one that contributed significantly to the internecine wars of the fifteenth century. This was recognized by successive sovereigns who attempted to legislate against abuses of the system, thereby reducing the effectiveness of the nobles' private armies and minimizing the threat of insurrection.

Badge knots of: 1. Heneage and 2. Hungerford. 3. The ape's clog badge of William de la Pole, Duke of Suffolk. 4. The Bourchier knot. 5. Crested helm and shield of arms of Sir Walter de Hungerford, from his seal of 1432. 6. The white lion badge of Mowbray and the black bull's head badge of Hastings shown as livery badges. 7. The Stafford knot

Badges

The uniforms worn by armed retinues and retainers were not necessarily composed of the colours of their lords' coats of arms: Lord William de Hastings' retainers wore purple and blue, for example, but his arms were a black *maunch* (a stylized sleeve) on silver. Similarly, the liveries of John Mowbray, Duke of Norfolk (d. 1476) were 'dark blew and tawny' but his arms were red and white – *Gules a Lion rampant Argent* (*see* page 57).

Badges were issued in conjunction with liveries to be worn on uniforms and borne on livery flags (*see* page 60). Many badges were simply charges taken from a shield of arms (the white lion of Mowbray, for example) while others were devices adopted for their hidden meaning or in allusion to a name, title or office. Typical are the mill-sail device of the lords Willoughby, the gold 'drag' (sledge) of the Lords Stourton, the silver ape's clog of William de la Pole, Duke of Suffolk and various stylized knots, the most familiar being that of the lords Stafford. Many badges were also used as crests (the black bull's head of Hastings, for example) and several chimerical creatures which began life as badges were later translated into heraldic supporters (*see* page 84).

The fifteenth century De Vere earls of Oxford used a number of badges which included the silver star (*mullet*) from their arms; a blue boar with gold tusks and bristles, which was also the De Vere crest; an enigmatic *cranket* device, which was probably a political allusion; and a bottle with a blue cord which may have been a pun on the family name (*de verre* being 'of glass'), though elsewhere this has been attributed to the office of Lord High Chamberlain which was held by John de Vere, Earl of Oxford (*c*. 1443–1513).

Such devices were sometimes combinations of badges obtained through marriage and seigniorial alliances or adopted for political purposes. The famous bear 'chained to the ragged staff' of Richard Nevill, Earl of Warwick ('Kingmaker'), is perhaps the most familiar example of two badges forming a single device (*see* page 64); while the combined falcon and fetterlock (manacle) badges of the dukes of York signified the frustrated political aspirations of that house. It was not until Edward, Duke of York (1442–83) became King of England in 1461 that the fetterlock was unclasped and the falcon of York no longer confined.

Many badges were translated into crests: Sir Walter de Hungerford, for instance, combined his badges of a sickle and a Hungerford knot with the *garb* (wheatsheaf) of the Peverels when he married the co-heiress of Thomas Peverel. Lord Hungerford's seal of 1432 shows two of these devices combined and borne as a crest: *A Garb between two Sickles* (*see* page 57).

1. Falcon and fetterlock badge of Richard Plantagenet, Duke of York
2. The de Vere cranket device
3. The black bull's head of Hastings
4. Sir Walter de Hungerford's sickle and garb device
5. Drag badge of the Lord Stourton
6. Mill sail device of the Lords Willoughby
7. de Vere's bottle with a blue cord

Heraldic Flags

In the early Middle Ages military command flags were simple triangular or swallow-tailed lance pennons on which were emblazoned a knight's arms. By the end of the twelfth century senior commanders were using rectangular banners, which were twice as high as they were wide, and by the fourteenth century these had developed into the now familiar square banners of the medieval nobility, the smaller banneret being reserved for the knights banneret who ranked between barons and knights bachelor.

The pennon (which measured about 1 metre (3 feet) in length) remained the flag of the knight bachelor whose promotion in the field of battle could be signified by the removal of the tails from his pennon, thereby forming the small banner of a banneret. Whether this was normal practice is uncertain but it is known that several knights, including Sir John Chandos (1367), were promoted in this way (*see* page 43).

Banners, bannerets and pennons were essentially the personal flags of nobility and knighthood, indicative of a man's hereditary superiority and of his presence in the field of battle. But, whereas the banner served to identify the person of a commander, it became impossible for large retinues to follow a single flag, particularly during the fourteenth and fifteenth centuries when armies were composed of numerous private and mercenary units. The mustering and rallying functions were therefore assigned to livery flags: notably the standard and guidon which bore the liveries and badges familiar to retainers and soldiery, and of which their uniforms were composed.

The greatest of the medieval livery flags, the long, tapering standard, served as a mustering point for feudal retainers during military campaigns and at tournaments. It carried a magnate's liveries and badges, and sometimes his motto and the national emblem – the cross of St George, for example. The medieval standard was usually about 2.4 metres (8 feet) long, but the Tudor heralds determined that flags of specific lengths should be prescribed to different ranks of the nobility: 'The Great Standard to be sette before the Kinges pavilion or tent – not to be borne in battel' was 10 metres (33 feet) long. A duke's standard was 6 metres (21 feet) in length, and that of a humble knight 3.5 metres (12 feet). Also known as the ancient, maintenance of the medieval standard was the responsibility of an officer of that name. Naval standards (known as streamers) were pointed or swallow-tailed and the motto and national device were usually omitted. The guidon was a small version of the standard, carried before a troop of retained men and essential as a rallying point in battle. Guidons were composed of the livery colours and usually bore a single badge and a national emblem but no motto.

Banner of the arms of Vaughan

13C banner of
Simon de Montfort

Banner of the arms of
West Dorset District Council

English Tudor guidon
of 'Mayster' Compton

Scottish standard of the Earls of Douglas with the
saltire of St Andrew at the hoist

The standard of Henry de Stafford featuring
the Stafford knot and the white swan of Bohun

Livery Collars

Collars, mantles and other insignia of the Order of the Garter are much in evidence in monumental brasses and effigies, as are Lancastrian and Yorkist livery collars.

The famous but enigmatic collar of esses (usually written SS) is of obscure origin. A chain of links, each in the form of the letter S, it was probably given as livery by 'time-honoured Lancaster', John of Gaunt (1340–99), and by Henry Bolingbroke who distributed 192 collars of SS among his retainers following his return from exile in 1399. As Henry IV, Bolingbroke later determined that 'all the sons of the king, dukes, earls, barons … might use the livery of our Lord the King of his collar as well in his absence as in his presence; and all other knights and esquires should use it only in the presence of the King'. He also used a device of linked esses as a personal badge (this appears in the effigy of his queen at Canterbury) and it has been suggested that both badge and collar alluded to the initial letter of his motto 'Sovereygne'.

At that time the Lancastrian collar appears to have comprised a strip of leather or velvet set with silver-gilt SS and terminating in two buckles linked by an ornamental trefoil from which a badge (such as the swan of Bohun) could be suspended. There are examples of SS letters in a variety of shapes, sizes and styles, sometimes reversed or horizontal, and set at varying distances from each other. In early versions of the collar the SS appear to have been attached to the material, possibly by rivets, and the collar fitted tightly over the camail when worn with armour. Later collars were made entirely of metal with the SS elaborately strung or linked together.

The collar of SS remained a Lancastrian device for over fifty years and was adopted by the Tudors who alternated the Lancastrian SS with Beaufort portcullises and added a Tudor Rose or portcullis as a pendant. Tudor SS collars were generally more substantial and were essentially chains of office rather than symbols of allegiance or decorations of honour. Today the collar is worn by kings of arms, heralds and serjeants at arms and, in modified form, by the Lord Chief Justice and the Lord Mayor of London.

The corresponding Yorkist collars are composed of alternate suns and roses with a white lion pendant (for Mortimer) or, under Richard III, white roses en soleil (surrounded by the rays of the sun) with a pendant of a white boar. There are nearly 100 examples of effigies and brasses with Yorkist collars but, of these, only one has a boar pendant, that of Sir Ralph Fitzherbert at Norbury in Derbyshire.

Lancastrian collar of SS with a swan pendant

Yorkist collar of suns and white roses with a lion pendant

Sir Edmund de Thorpe. Effigy with collar of SS, *c.* 1418

Sir Thomas More's collar, from a painting by Holbein

Yorkist collar of suns and roses. A detail of the carved effigy of Sir Henry Pierrepoint

The Kingmaker

The arms and badges of Richard Nevill, Earl of Warwick and of Salisbury (1428–71), provide vivid evidence of the potency of heraldry in the fifteenth century.

Richard Nevill the elder (1400–60), a younger son of Ralph, Earl of Westmorland (d. 1425), bore his paternal arms (*Gules a Saltire Argent*) which, as a cadet, he differenced with a label of three points in the Lancastrian colours of silver and blue – a reference to his mother, Joan Beaufort (d. 1440), who was the legitimated daughter of John of Gaunt.

On the death of Thomas Montagu, Earl of Salisbury, in 1428, Richard inherited the Salisbury and Monthermer titles and arms through his wife, who was Earl Thomas's heir (*Quarterly Argent three Fusils conjoined in fess Gules and Gold an Eagle displayed Vert*) and these he quartered with precedence before his own paternal coat.

Richard's son, also Richard (who came to be known as 'Kingmaker'), inherited this combined coat to which he added the accumulated quarterings of the earldom of Warwick acquired through his marriage with Anne, heiress of Richard Beauchamp, Earl of Warwick (d. 1439). These quarterings included the arms of Beauchamp (*Gules a Fess between six Crosses crosslets Gold*), those of the former Newburgh earls of Warwick (*Chequy Gold and Blue a Chevron Ermine*) and the arms of Clare (*Gold three Chevronels Gules*) and Despencer (*Quarterly Argent and Gules in the second and third quarters a Fret Gold and overall a Bend Sable*) which Richard Beauchamp had acquired through his second wife, Isabella, daughter and heir of Thomas Despencer, Earl of Gloucester and a descendant of Gilbert de Clare.

Richard Nevill used only his paternal arms on his shield, but his banner and horse caparison would have been emblazoned with the quarterings of the accumulated lordships through which he exercised his power. The senior of these (Warwick and Salisbury) he placed in the first and second quarters, with Nevill in the third and Despencer in the fourth. He used two crests, a white swan's head and neck rising from a red coronet (for Warwick) and a demi-griffin issuing from a coronet (for Salisbury), and his other devices included the now familiar chained bear and ragged staff.

These badges, derived from the Beauchamp earls of Warwick, were used individually or in combination on the scarlet liveries of Nevill's retainers and on his standards and guidons:

> Claim thou the crown, and set thy standard up
> And in the same advance the milk-white rose,
> And then to guard it will I rouse the bear,
> Inviron'd with ten thousand ragged staves.
>
> Shakespeare, *Henry VI Part 2*, Scene 2.

Shields of Arms of English Knights
at the
Battle of Agincourt

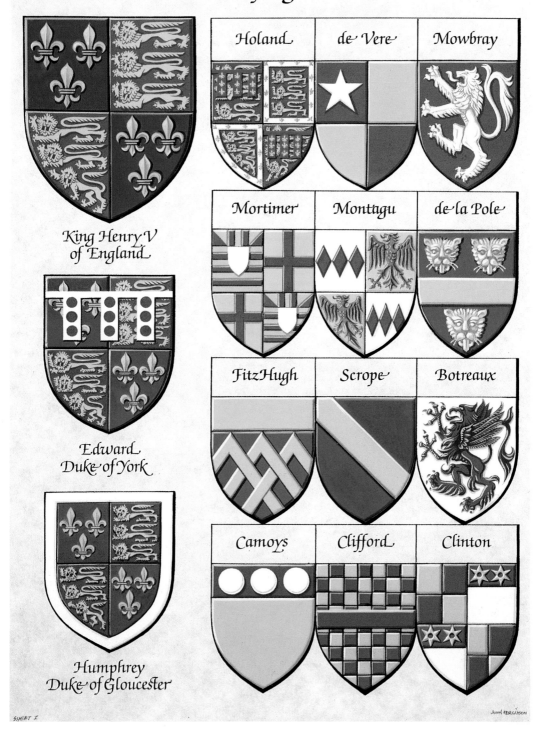

King Henry V
of England

Edward
Duke of York

Humphrey
Duke of Gloucester

Holand

de Vere

Mowbray

Mortimer

Montagu

de la Pole

FitzHugh

Scrope

Botreaux

Camoys

Clifford

Clinton

Shields of Arms of English Knights
at the
Battle of Agincourt

The Banner of St George

The Banner of St Edward

The Banner of St Edmund

Ros

Talbot

Willoughby

Harrington

Bourchier

Cornwall

Grey

Umfraville

Erpingham

Babthorpe

Cheney

Strickland

Sheet II

John Ferguson

PLATE 2

Shields of Arms of English Knights
at the
Battle of Agincourt

Woodstock Standard of King Henry V

Kyghley	Gamme	de Thorpe	Codrington

Ferrers	Le Boteler	Phellip	Robsert

Antelope Standard of King Henry V

JOHN FERGUSON

PLATE 3

PLATE 4 **Effigial Figures** Conjectural designs based on heraldry in the late fourteenth–century cloister vault of Canterbury Cathedral.

PLATE 5 **Heraldic Flags** 1. 15C. banner of the arms of Fitzhugh.
2. Medieval lance pennons. 3. Guidon of the badge and liveries of
William de Hastings d.1483. 4. Modern clan chieftain's standard
(Erskine). 5. Banner of Sir Walter Hungerford. 6. A royal badge
banner of the Tudor period. 7. Gonfannon of the arms and livery
colours of the Worshipful Company of Grocers.

LANCASTER

CALNE

CHESTER

ABINGDON

PLATE 7   The arms of the Borough of Weymouth and Melcombe Regis in Dorset, granted in 1592. The banners commemorate Edward I, from whom Melcombe Regis received its first charter, and his wife Eleanor of Castile. *(Courtesy of the Mayor and Corporation of Weymouth and reproduced by kind permission of the Museum, Brewer's Quay, Weymouth.)*

PLATE 6   **Civic Arms** *Opposite, top left:* the arms of Lancaster, Lancashire, which were confirmed in 1907 (when the crest and supporters were also granted), include references to the royal heraldry of Edmund, first Earl of Lancaster and son of Henry III. The famous red rose of Lancaster was derived from the golden rose of the Earl's mother, Eleanor of Provence. 'Loyne' is a form of Lune, the river from which the city takes its name. The town of Lancaster, Massachusetts, bears similar arms. *Top right:* the feathers in the arms of Calne, Wiltshire, are those of the heir apparent to the English throne and recall that the town was once part of the Duchy of Cornwall. The crest (granted, with supporters, in 1950) commemorates a disastrous meeting of the witan in 978 when 'the oldest counsellors of England fell at Calne from an upper floor', only Archbishop Dunstan escaping injury by standing on a beam. *Bottom left:* confirmed in 1580, the arms of Chester dimidiate the royal arms of England with those of the Earls of Chester. Hugh Lupus, the first Earl (created 1071), is commemorated in the punning wolf supporter (Latin, *lupus* = wolf). *Bottom right:* the medieval arms of Abingdon, Berkshire, are similar to those of the former Abbey, while the crest and supporters were granted as recently as 1962.

PLATE 8 **Arms, Coronets and Insignia of Peers** *Top left:* Robert Walpole, Earl of Orford, Knight Companion of the Most Noble Order of the Garter. *Top right:* Archibald Kennedy, Marquess of Ailsa and Knight of the Most Ancient and Most Noble Order of the Thistle. *Bottom left:* Baron Rawlinson, Knight Commander of the Most Honourable Order of the Bath. *Bottom right:* Baron D'Abernon, Knight Commander of the Most Distinguished Order of St Michael and St George.

Beauchamp

Montagu

Newburgh

Monthermer

The arms of Richard Nevill, Earl of Warwick

Crest of
Richard Beauchamp,
Earl of Warwick

Crest of
Richard Nevill,
Earl of Salisbury

The bear and staff standard of Richard Nevill

Ralph Nevill

Richard Nevill

Clare

Despenser

1. Henry Holland, Duke of Exeter
2. William Herbert, Earl of Pembroke
3. Sir John Fastolfe
4. Sir Thomas Gargrave
5. Thomas, Lord Clifford

But the 'roused bear' was soon to be cast down, for tradition tells how Warwick 'Kingmaker', in the mist-shrouded field of Barnet in 1471, mistook the Earl of Oxford's livery badge, a silver star, for the Yorkist white rose *en soleil* and ordered his men to charge at Oxford's contingent, believing them to be royal troops:

> The envious mist so much deceived the sight,
> That where eight hundred men, which valiant Oxford brought,
> Wore comets on their coats, great Warwick's force, which thought
> They had King Edward's been, which so with suns were drest,
> First made their shot at them, who, by their friends distrest,
> Constrained were to fly, being scatter'd here and there.
>
> Drayton, *Polyolbion*

As a consequence, Warwick was slain, Oxford fled the field 'and thereafter befell Tewkesbury, the murder of Henry VI, and the destruction of the House of Lancaster' (A. C. Fox-Davies).

6. John Talbot, Earl of
   Shrewsbury
7. John Talbot the younger,
   Viscount Lisle
8. Humphrey Stafford, Duke of
   Buckingham
9. John de Vere, Earl of Oxford
10. Sir Humphrey Stafford
11. William, Lord Hastings
12. Anthony Widville,
    Earl Rivers

Richard III

Heraldic devices provided a rich source of inspiration for the political
satirist. One of the best-known examples is the prophetic rhyme im-
prudently circulated by William Collingbourn, sometime sheriff of
Wiltshire and Dorset, prior to 1483:

> The Cat, the Rat, and Lovel our Dog
> Doe rule all England, under the Hog.
> The crooke backt boare the way hath found
> To root our roses from the ground;
> Both flower and bud will he confound,
> Till king of beasts the same be crown'd:
> And then the dog, the cat, and rat,
> Shall in his trough feed and be fat.

The hog was Richard of Gloucester (later Richard III) whose badge was a
white boar (*sanglier*) with gold tusks and bristles; the cat was Sir William
Catesby whose device was a white cat spotted with black and wearing a
gold collar; the rat was Sir Richard Ratcliff and the dog, Francis, Lord
Lovel whose crest was a silver wolf-dog (*lupellus* – an allusion to his name)
and his badge a gold padlock. The roses were, of course, the members of
the royal house whom Gloucester was alleged to have eliminated. Collingbourn paid dearly for his impertinence: he was arrested and executed.

The origin of Gloucester's infamous device, the 'wretched, bloody and
usurping boar' of Shakespeare, remains a mystery though it has been
suggested (somewhat tentatively by Planché) that it was a pun on the
name Ebor for York and was, therefore, adopted or inherited in allusion to
his father's dukedom of York. Richard, both as Duke of Gloucester and
later as king, was certainly very fond of the badge which appeared on his
standards, together with the white rose *en soleil* device of the House of
York, and in his arms as supporters. His pursuivant was called *Blanc
Sanglier*, as was one of his favourite war-horses.

Following his bloody death at Bosworth in 1485, Richard's white boar
was everywhere 'rased and plucked doune' though it did not disappear
entirely from the heraldic scene. Despite vilification by the Tudors, the
patronage of the former Duke of Gloucester was commemorated in a
number of civic grants of arms, notably that of 1538 to the City of
Gloucester (*see* page 131). More recently, a white boar has been granted as
a crest in the arms of the Richard III Society.

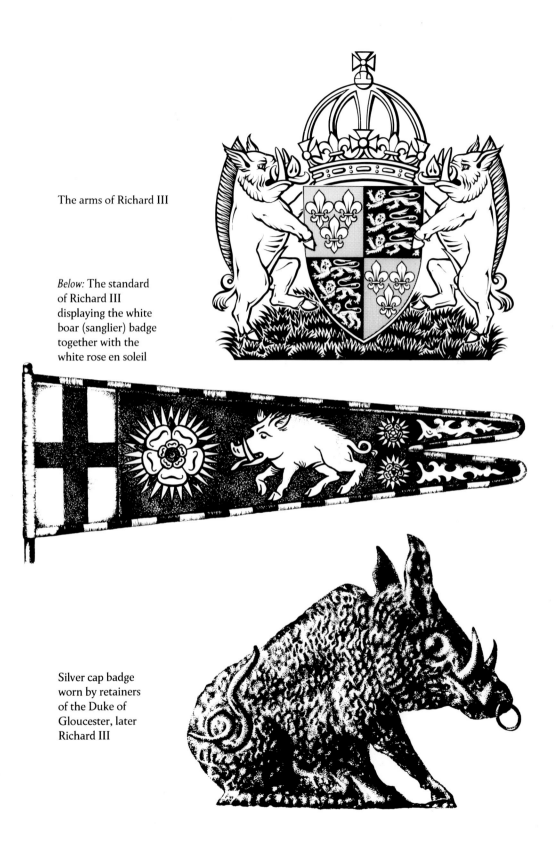

The arms of Richard III

Below: The standard of Richard III displaying the white boar (sanglier) badge together with the white rose en soleil

Silver cap badge worn by retainers of the Duke of Gloucester, later Richard III

The College of Arms

For students of English heraldry (armorists), Richard III is best remembered for his founding of the College of Arms.

The term is now most readily associated with the heralds' splendid building in Queen Victoria Street, London, but the College founded by Richard in 1484 was (and remains) a body corporate comprising the Officers of Arms in Ordinary who exercise heraldic authority on behalf of the sovereign and are members of the Royal Household.

Royal officers of arms had conducted their affairs as a corporate body since the early fifteenth century but, prior to 1484, were not formally incorporated. In that year the heralds were also granted, in perpetual succession, the use of a house named Coldharbour in the parish of All Hallows the Less in the City of London. But, after Bosworth, all grants made by Richard III were revoked by Henry VII's Act of Resumption and Coldharbour was given to the new king's mother, Margaret, Countess of Richmond. As a consequence, the College's records and manuscripts were transferred to the home of John Wrythe, Garter King of Arms, and by 1504 they appear to have been dispersed among various officers of arms who had adopted the chapter house of the Black Friars as their headquarters.

The College was re-incorporated in July, 1555 and 'The Kings, Heralds and Pursuivants of the Corporation of the Office of Arms, London' received Derby House, near St Paul's Cathedral, as a residence. Derby House was destroyed in the Great Fire of 1666 though its records and manuscripts were saved. It was not until December, 1671 that new letters patent were obtained from Charles II and the heralds were able to effect 'fitte meanes' to invite subscriptions and the 'voluntary benevolence' of the nobility and gentry in order to build a new residence on the site of the old. The building was quadrangular but the subsequent construction of Queen Victoria Street (c. 1870) resulted in the demolition of the southern wing.

The College building is owned and governed by a chapter comprising the thirteen officers of arms (known collectively as the heralds), presided over by Garter King of Arms, and contains the High Court of Chivalry, the heralds' chambers and a magnificent collection of heraldic and genealogical records and documents.

The Earl Marshal exercises jurisdiction over the officers of arms but is not a member of the body corporate and enjoys only 'visitorial powers'.

The official records of the College are maintained in the Records Room but are not available for public inspection. An Officer in Waiting is on duty to receive enquiries from the public and, though the officers of arms have private practices, their principal responsibilities remain those of ceremonial officers to the Crown.

Armorial bearings of the College of Arms

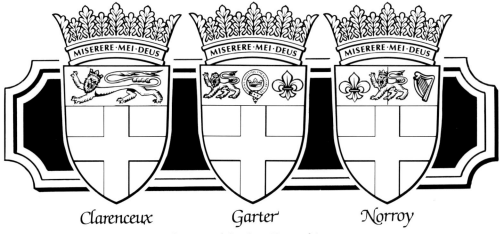

Clarenceux   Garter   Norroy

The arms of the three Kings of Arms

The High Court of Chivalry

In the early days of heraldry, coats of arms were assumed by the knightly class, often with the advice of heralds, but without regulation. In order that the adoption of heraldic devices should be controlled, the High Court of Chivalry was established in the early fourteenth century as the Court of the Constable and Marshal, having jurisdiction over all matters armorial. Following the execution of Edward Stafford, Duke of Buckingham and Constable of England in 1521, the office of Constable became vacant and has remained so except for special occasions such as coronations. The Marshal has therefore sat alone in the Court of Chivalry (though in practice a surrogate is usually appointed) and exercises sole jurisdiction over the officers of arms in matters of heraldry, honour and precedence. The title was originally Marshal but is now Earl Marshal and Hereditary Marshal of England and is vested in the dukes of Norfolk. The Marshal, who held the senior military rank beneath the sovereign, was responsible for marshalling the various contingents of the royal army (assisted by the heralds who were familiar with magnatial liveries and badges) and this function is commemorated in the gold and black staffs of office in the Norfolk arms. Today, the Earl of Marshal is the great officer of state responsible for state ceremonies (but not 'royal' occasions such as weddings) and hereditary judge in the Court of Chivalry which is also called the Court of the Earl Marshal.

The Law of Arms is not common law but civil law, and the Court of Chivalry is, therefore, a civil court. Those records that have survived from the late medieval period demonstrate clearly that a right to arms could be established only by proof of a grant from a lawful authority (i.e. a king of arms acting on the authority of the sovereign, or the sovereign himself) or by descent from one who had borne arms from time immemorial which, in the Court of Chivalry, was deemed to be 1066. During the heralds' visitations of the seventeenth century a claim with proof of a prescriptive use of arms from the beginning of the reign of Elizabeth I (1558) was considered to be sufficient.

There are few records of proceedings before the late seventeenth century when the Court experienced a period of frenetic activity. At that time the King's Advocate (the equivalent of the Attorney General), who prosecuted alleged offenders, set out articles detailing charges and cited case law – a practice which had hitherto been almost unknown in the Court of Chivalry. After 1737 the Court did not sit until a test case was brought in 1954 at which it was established that, despite a lapse of over two hundred years, the Court's authority was still valid.

Howard

Brotherton

Warren

Fitzalan

The arms of the
Duke of Norfolk, Earl
Marshal and Hereditary
Marshal of England

Officers of Arms

It is uncertain when the first English royal heralds were appointed. The earliest known reference occurs in 1276 when 'a King of Heralds North of Trent' is mentioned, but the first occasion on which a herald is described by reference to a specific title of office was in 1327 when Carlisle Herald was created by Edward III – though even then it is not clear whether this was an exclusively royal office. It is evident that, at that time, officers of arms moved from private to royal service (and vice versa), titles of office were often abandoned and then revived, and some royal and non-royal heralds possessed similar titles.

During the reign of Edward III (1327–77) Claroncel (or Clarencell), Norreys, Volant (or Vaillant), Falcon, Aquitaine and Guyenne kings of arms were appointed. Clarenceux and Norroy became the titles of the two English provincial kings of arms, but from 1380 to 1419 the king of the southern province of England was Leicester King of Arms and in the reigns of Henry V and Henry VI (1413–66) the Roy d'armes de North (i.e. north of the river Trent) was Lancaster. It is likely, therefore, that prior to 1420 in the south of England, and 1467 in the north, the kings of arms used their personal titles while their provinces were known as 'of the Clarenceux' and 'of the Norreys'.

The (English) Officers of Arms in Ordinary now comprise three kings of arms (Garter, Clarenceux and Norroy and Ulster), six heralds (Chester, Lancaster, Richmond, Somerset, Windsor and York) and four pursuivants (Bluemantle, Portcullis, Rouge Croix and Rouge Dragon). Only a king of arms has authority to grant armorial bearings and in England and Wales this is subject to the formal approval of the Earl Marshal in the form of a warrant. The Officers of Arms in Ordinary act as heraldic and genealogical consultants and charge fees for their advice and services; they are members of the Royal Household and receive (meagre) salaries of the sovereign. There are also Officers of Arms Extraordinary who, while not members of the body corporate, assist their brother officers on state and other occasions. They include Arundel, Beaumont, Maltravers, Norfolk, Surrey, Wales and New Zealand heralds and Fitzalan Pursuivant (*see* pages 102–4 for the Scottish and Irish heralds).

In England the prerequisites to a right to bear arms have never been defined but in practice a successful petitioner must be perceived to be a 'gentleman' and the kings of arms are authorized, by their letters patent of appointment, to grant arms to 'eminent men' (which phrase includes, of course, women and corporate bodies). Armorial bearings are still granted by means of signed letters patent to which the seals of the granting kings of arms are appended (*see* colour plate 16).

Badges of the English Heralds and Pursuivants

1. Lancaster Herald. 2. York Herald. 3. Richmond Herald.
4. Somerset Herald. 5. Rouge Dragon Pursuivant.
6. Portcullis Pursuivant. 7. Rouge Croix Pursuivant.
8. Chester Herald. 9. Bluemantle Pursuivant.
10. Windsor Herald.

Bosworth Field

On 7 August 1485 Henry Tudor, Earl of Richmond, landed at Mill Bay
near St Ann's Head in Pembrokeshire with 2,000 troops – not regular men-
at-arms or even mercenaries but 'the sweepings of the gaols of Normandy'
(Ross) – and a decidedly tenuous claim to the English throne, his Welsh
ancestry proclaimed in the dragon standard of Cadwalladar. Richard III
and Tudor met on the plain of Redemore near Dadlington in Leicestershire
on 22 August. Treachery and procrastination ruled the day and Richard was
hacked to death at Tudor's feet, having staked his crown on a final heroic
charge aimed at direct confrontation with the 'accursed Tydder'.

Richard III remains the most enigmatic and, to many, charismatic
of English sovereigns and his death at Bosworth Field symbolized the
denouement of the Age of Chivalry.

The chronicler, Hall, describes how, after the battle, Richard's naked
corpse was 'trussed behynde a persivaunt of arms called *Blaunche Sanglier*
or whyte bore, lyke a hogge or calfe, the hed and armes hangynge on the
one syde of the horse, and the legges on the other syde, and all bysprynckled
with myre and bloude … When his death was knowen, the proude
braggyng whyte bore was violently rased and plucked doune from every
signe and place where it myght be espied, so yll was his lyfe that men
wished the memorie of hym to be buried with his carren corps.' Henry
Tudor entered London and 'with great pompe and triumphe he roade
through the Cytie to the cathedral churche of S. Paule, wher he offered his
standardes. In the one was the ymage of S. George, in the second was the
red firye dragon beaten upon white and grene sarcenet, the third was of
yelowe tarterne, in the whyche was paynted a dunne cowe [a dun cow –
Henry's badge as Earl of Richmond].'

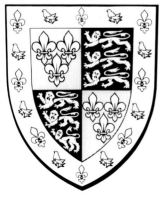

Henry Tudor

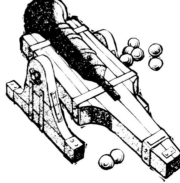

Jasper Tudor

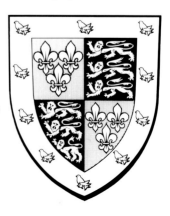

BOSWORTH FIELD
22 August 1485

The 'Red firye dragon beaten upon white and green sarcenet' standard of Henry Tudor

The shields of arms of some of the participants at the Battle of Bosworth Field:

1. Sir William Stanley. 2. Sir Richard Ratcliff.
3. Sir William Brandon (standard bearer to Henry of Richmond). 4. Sir Reginald Bray who recovered Richard III's crown after the battle. 5. Sir John Howard, the Earl Marshal of England. 6. Sir John Cheyney.
7. Viscount Lovel. 8. Sir Robert Brackenbury, Lieutenant of the Tower.

The arms of Henry VII impaling those
of Elizabeth of York

The crowned hawthorn
device of Henry VII

Versions of the Tudor Rose

Panel from the gates of Henry VII's
Chapel at Westminster

4   The Heraldry of the Decadence

Historically, the red rose has come to represent the concept of parliamentary sanction by which Henry VII acceded to the English throne. But in order that his descendants should enjoy an inalienable right of succession, he married Elizabeth of York – the heiress of the white rose.

The impaled arms of Henry and Elizabeth reflect this political reconciliation of parliamentary and legitimist principles. To the royal arms (*Quarterly France and England*) were added those of Mortimer (*Gold three Bars Azure on a Chief of the first two Pallets between two Gyrons of the second and over all an Escutcheon Argent*) and Ulster (*Gold a Cross Gules*) and, because Elizabeth was a daughter of Edward IV, the royal arms occur again in the first quarter.

Similarly, the rival roses were combined in the beautiful Tudor Rose that was to become the universal symbol of the Tudor dynasty and of the new administration:

> These roses sprang and budded faire, and carried such a grace,
> That Kings of England in their armes afford them worthy place,
> And flourish may these roses long that all the world may tell
> The owners of these princely flowers in virtues doe excell.

Henry Tudor's victory at Bosworth was commemorated in his device of a crowned hawthorn bush, his Welsh ancestry in the red dragon of Cadwalladar (from whom the Tudors claimed descent) and his Beaufort blood in the portcullis badge (*see* page 75) derived through his mother, the Lancastrian heiress, Lady Margaret Beaufort – all borne on liveries of white and green. More than ever before, membership of the Order of the Garter became an instrument of political and diplomatic influence: Tudor roses were incorporated in the insignia of the Order and to the collar was added a pendant of St George and the Dragon – 'the champion of ordered government striking down the monster of anarchy' (Scott-Giles) (*see* pages 120–1).

Henry recognized the potency of visual symbolism but, while Tudor devices became ubiquitous in the architectural decoration, furnishings, window glass and manuscripts of the period, the use of magnatial badges for political and military purposes declined as the practice of livery and maintenance was rigorously suppressed (*see* page 56).

Henry VIII

There were as many versions of the royal arms during Henry VIII's reign (1509–47) as there were queens. The arms of Catherine of Aragon included the allusive quarterings of Castile and Leon, the impaled arms of Aragon and Sicily and, in the base of the shield, the pomegranate device of Granada. Henry's personal and political affinity with Spain was further emphasized in his choice of badges: the Tudor Rose dimidiating a sheaf of silver arrows (for Aragon) and combined with the pomegranate of Granada – to produce a strange botanical hybrid. Henry prosecuted his ancestral claim to the French throne with the support of his father-in-law, King Ferdinand of Spain, the Emperor Maximilian and the Pope, and it was at this time that he was granted the title *Fidei Defensor* (Defender of the Faith) which is still used by his Protestant successors.

Following the Great Divorce, Henry was acutely aware of his new queen's humble origins. Anne Bullen's paternal arms, *Argent* [silver] *a Chevron Gules* [red] *between three Bull's heads couped Sable* [black], clearly referred to the name Bullen (or Boleyn) and were quartered with a number of inconspicuous families. Before her marriage, and to mark her creation as Marchioness of Pembroke, Anne was obliged to abandon her father's arms in favour of a complex shield which included the arms of Lancaster, Angoulême, Guienne, Butler, Rochfort, Brotherton and Warrenne – a distinguished collection of quarterings but also a decidedly spurious one! It is interesting to note that, while the pomegranate and arrow sheaf devices of Queen Catherine came to symbolize resistance to the divorce and, thereby, English Catholicism (both were later adopted by Queen Mary), Queen Anne's badge of a silver falcon holding a sceptre became an emblem of Protestantism and was inherited by Elizabeth I (*see* page 89).

To Queen Jane, his third wife, the King granted honorific arms in which the royal lions and *fleurs-de-lis* were re-arranged in a single shield and quartered with the arms of Seymour: *Gules* [red] *two Wings conjoined in lure Gold*. The phoenix crest of the Seymour family commemorates their royal ancestor who died after giving birth to the future Edward VI.

Queen Katherine, Henry's fifth wife, received two augmentations of honour each of which she quartered with the illustrious arms of Howard. One was blue with three gold *fleurs-de-lis* between ermine *flaunches*, each charged with a red rose, and the other was blue with two gold lions and four half *fleurs-de-lis*.

Katherine Parr was also granted an augmented shield of arms, *Gold on a Pile between six Roses Gules* [red] *three Roses Argent* [silver], and this she impaled with her paternal arms: *Argent* [silver] *two Bars Azure* [blue] *within a Bordure engrailed Sable* [black].

Arms of Henry VIII and Queen
Catherine of Aragon

Arms of Henry VIII and Queen
Anne Bullen

Tudor Rose and Pomegranate of Granada

Paternal arms of Anne Bullen

Tudor Rose and Silver Arrows
of Aragon

Badge of Katherine Parr

Left: Jane Seymour   *Centre:* Katherine Howard   *Right:* Catherine Parr impaling her paternal arms

Ecclesiastical Magnates

The archbishops, bishops and royal abbots of the Middle Ages were ecclesiastical magnates, many of whom held office as privy advisers in the King's Council, the *Curia Regis*. Many accomplished clerics were elevated to the great Offices of State and their services rewarded with the emoluments of a bishopric – a device by which the Crown was spared the payment of a substantial salary and pension.

Unique among the Lords Spiritual were the prince bishops of Durham who were appointed as counts palatine, head of church and state in a vast territory that included St Cuthbert's seventh-century bishopric of Lindisfarne. The Great Seal of the prince bishops depicted an enthroned figure of a bishop and, on the reverse, the bishop as an equestrian figure in full armour. By the fourteenth century the Palatinate was at the height of its military power and its warrior-bishops are uniquely commemorated in the plumed mitre enfiling a ducal coronet above their arms. Their authority was reduced under the Tudor kings but, even so, in 1585 the Bishop of Durham remained the largest land-holder in England.

Although, prior to the Reformation, most bishops were elected by chapter, it was usual for the Pope formally to confirm the appointment of a king's nominee, a decision which was then ratified by chapter. One effect of this system was that prominent members of the royal household were frequently appointed as bishops and members of the *curia regis*. The extraordinary influence of these few families, in matters ecclesiastical and secular, is evident in the ubiquity of their personal arms alongside those of the offices they held.

Cardinals, who belonged to the highest ecclesiastical rank, displayed above their arms a scarlet ecclesiastical hat: a domed hat of felt with a wide brim from which depend cords, interlaced with gold thread, and tassels. These hats, which were worn by cardinals for official engagements, were instituted by Pope Innocent IV in the thirteenth century.

Thomas Wolsey (c. 1474–1530), the son of an Ipswich butcher, whose elevation to archbishop, cardinal and Lord Chancellor, reflected his domination of foreign and domestic policy under Henry VIII, adopted singularly grandiose arms. In these were combined the arms of the ancient earls of Suffolk, the silver *engrailed* cross of Ufford and the leopard's heads of De la Pole. Clearly, Wolsey's arms were intended to add lustre to his East Anglian origins, though he was related to neither of the former earls. On the cross he placed a red lion, probably a reference to Pope Leo X from whom he received his cardinalate, and on a gold chief a red rose between two Becket birds (Cornish choughs) in allusion to his illustrious namesake and predecessor, Thomas Becket.

1. The banner of arms of Cardinal Wolsey as Archbishop of York and Chancellor of England. An illustration taken from a design in *Prince Arthur's Book*. 2. Arms of the bishops of Durham with the plumed mitre enfiling a ducal coronet indicating the Palatinate jurisdiction. 3. The personal arms of John Fordham, Bishop of Durham, 1382–8

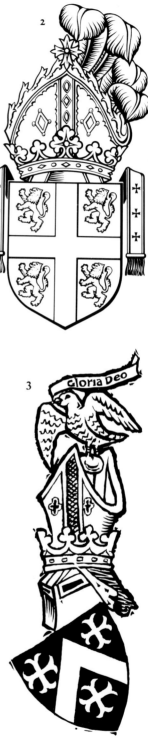

Heraldic Supporters

Supporters are figures, usually beasts, creatures or of human form, that appear to 'support' the shield in a coat of arms. Unlike the other elements of a coat of arms, heraldic supporters have no practical origin. It has been suggested that they may have originated in the flamboyant practice of disguising retainers as beasts and chimerical creatures at pageants and tournaments but there are more plausible explanations.

In the thirteenth and fourteenth centuries, creatures were often depicted in the interstices of seals (*see* pages 21 and 49) and as such may reasonably be considered to be the precursors of heraldic supporters, even though their function was essentially decorative. Other seals show a shield of arms suspended from a creature by means of a guige or strap: in the seal of Humphrey de Bohun (1322), for example, where the guige is carried by the black swan of the earls of Hereford, and in the seal of Thomas Holland, Earl of Kent (1380), in which the shield is suspended from the neck of a white hind.

Many of these creatures had been adopted by medieval magnates for use as badges on their liveries and to mark personal possessions and, by the fifteenth century, even the lesser nobility would have accumulated several through inheritance and marriage. These were often translated into crests and, later, into supporters. In most early examples, the two supporters were alike but there are also single supporters, notably in Scottish heraldry where an *eagle displayed* ['spread-eagled'] is not uncommon.

As the practical application of heraldry declined, so the complexity of the stylized coat of arms increased and, by the late Tudor period, the use of crests and supporters was subject to regulation and control. Today, supporters are symbols of eminence granted only to peers, knights of the Garter and Thistle, and to the most senior ranks of the British orders of chivalry including the Most Venerable Order of the Hospital of St John of Jerusalem. With the exception of hereditary peers, supporters are not transmitted to heirs. In Scotland, supporters may also be granted by Lord Lyon King of Arms, the senior herald, to certain knights, clan chiefs and the heirs of minor barons who sat in Parliament prior to 1587. In both countries, certain families claim a customary right to depict supporters in their arms even though they would not otherwise qualify, while others have been granted supporters by virtue of a royal warrant. Supporters may also be granted to bodies corporate, the criteria being eminence and permanence.

Most human figures are of comparatively recent date and sometimes look rather incongruous supporting a medieval shield and helmet: the diver and Mexican poet supporters of Lord Cowdray, for example, and the two electrical mechanics in the arms of Lord Ashfield.

The seal of Humphrey de Bohun
1322

One of a pair of identical
supporters from the arms of
Sir Hugh Vaughan granted in 1508

Seal of Thomas Holland, 1398

Sea-horse supporter from the arms of the city of
Newcastle-upon-Tyne, dating from 1575

The Heralds' Visitations

By the end of the fifteenth century, 'the bearing of coat armor' was so widely abused that it became necessary for the heralds to survey and record the devices and pedigrees of all those claiming armigerous status and to correct any irregularities.

In 1530, Clarenceux King of Arms was authorized to travel throughout his province (south of the river Trent), to enter all dwellings and churches and there to survey and record whatever arms he might find and 'to put down or otherwise deface at his discretion ... in plate, jewels, paper, parchment, windows, gravestones and monuments or elsewhere wheresoever they may be set or placed' those arms he found to be assumed unlawfully. He was also to denounce by proclamation all those who had usurped arms or titles such as knight, esquire or gentleman.

In practice, it was the heralds and the county sheriffs and their officers who conducted the visitations. Claimants were summoned to appear before the herald or his deputy at a specified time and place and to prove the authority by which their arms were borne. This might be by means of a pedigree, confirmation or grant which would be recorded by the herald who also sketched the arms in sufficient detail for them to be transferred to the manuscript volumes which now comprise the Visitation Books at the College of Arms. If the arms and pedigree were found to be in order they were confirmed. If they were lawful but in some way defective, corrections were made and recorded. If the herald was unable to approve the claim, the usurper was required to renounce any right to the title or arms and to sign a disclaimer. Those who ignored the directive could be summoned to appear before the Earl Marshal in the Court of Chivalry.

In England, major visitations took place in 1580, 1620 and 1666 and these resulted in a proliferation of grants of arms and crests to the new establishment: gentlemen who were concerned more with the administration of the state and the development of commerce than with the tournament or battlefield.

In Ireland, the social upheavals following the plantation schemes of the sixteenth and seventeenth centuries resulted in an influx of English and Scottish families many of whom were armigerous. The first Irish visitation took place in 1568 and was conducted by Ulster King of Arms whose office had been created just sixteen years earlier. Not only did the Irish visitations record and confirm arms and titles, they also served to establish the claims of gentry families previously unknown to the Ulster Office. From 1560 to 1690 heirs or executors were also obliged to provide a funeral certificate on which were recorded the arms and pedigree of a deceased armiger.

A typical page from a herald's visitation notebook of about 1580

Elizabeth I and Mary Queen of Scots

Minor changes to the royal arms of Elizabeth I (1558–1603) reflected the magnificence of Gloriana's reign and the mystique of the Virgin Queen. Both the red dragon of Cadwallader and the red mantling of the medieval kings were lavishly gilded to match the golden lions and *fleurs-de-lis* of England and France.

But it was in the matter of the succession that heraldry was to play a significant political role. Elizabeth retained the French lilies in her arms, thereby perpetuating her ancestors' claim to the French throne, but she was singularly exercised when others did likewise. The male line of the English royal house had expired with Edward VI and the legitimist heir was Mary, Queen of Scots. Others considered Mary to be a coheiress with Katherine Grey, the sister of Lady Jane and a descendant of Henry VII's younger daughter. Both women were entitled to quarter the royal arms of England but while Mary did so without compunction, Katherine diplomatically used the Beaufort arms (*see* page 1).

Mary (quite properly) quartered her arms as Queen of Scots with those of England but, on her marriage with the French Dauphin, she displayed the English royal arms on an escutcheon of pretence, a small shield at the centre of her husband's arms. In heraldry, this form of marshalling is indicative of an heraldic heiress and by adopting it Mary effectively declared herself to be the true heir to the English throne. The Dauphin succeeded as Francis II and, on his death, Mary dimidiated [halved] her widow's shield (including the escutcheon of pretence) with her own. This was not normal heraldic practice and, again, was meant to emphasize her claim to be Elizabeth's heiress. The English heralds pronounced: 'we find the same prejudicial unto the Queen's Majesty' and the articles drawn up in 1572 against Mary recited in detail the marshalling of her arms which, in Elizabeth's eyes, compounded her offence. The significance of Mary's arms should not be under-estimated. Had Henry VIII's divorce of Catherine of Aragon proved invalid, Elizabeth would have been illegitimate and Mary the true Queen of England.

Among Elizabeth's badges were her mother's silver falcon, a crowned rose, a phoenix which supposedly celebrated her recovery from smallpox, and a sieve device, the meaning of which still eludes us. Queen Mary adopted numerous devices including a Wheel of Fortune on which two women carried a war-like lance (Elizabeth) and a cornucopia (Mary); a caged bird (Mary) above which hovered a hawk (Elizabeth) with the words 'It is ill with me now and I fear worst betides me'; and a sun (Mary) eclipsed by the moon (Elizabeth) and the motto 'She taketh the light she envies'.

The arms of Queen Elizabeth I

Mary, Queen of Scots.
Arms as wife of the Dauphin
of France

Falcon badge
of Elizabeth I

Mary, Queen of Scots.
Arms after the death of
Francis II

Heraldic Decadence

During the late and post-Tudor period (now known as The Heraldry of the Decadence), armorial practice degenerated. 'By the sixteenth century the heralds had taught all men that the shield of arms was the symbol and voucher of gentility, and that, without one, wealth was ignoble' (Oswald Barron). The practical application of armory in the battlefield and tournament was replaced by an almost obsessional preoccupation with pomp and panoply, exaggerated ceremonial and 'parchment heraldry'. Coats of arms became stylized, extravagant and often singularly unattractive while many crests of the period, perceived by the new gentility to be marks of particular distinction, would have looked quite ridiculous affixed to a helmet.

In such a climate, purveyors of illegal coats of arms were legion: in 1577 a warrant was issued for the arrest of one William Dawkyns for impersonating a Queen's officer, for selling coats of arms and compiling false pedigrees. He was brought before Star Chamber and was sentenced to be whipped and to lose his ears, as well as to be pilloried in every shire where he had transacted his 'noisome business'. Even the heralds were perceived by many to be venal. Ben Jonson, in his *Every Man Out of His Humour* (1599) describes how one Sogliardo procured for himself a coat of arms and the accompanying style of gentleman by paying substantial fees to a herald who devised for him arms depicting a headless (brainless) swine. Jonson was clearly irritated by the prospect of so many counterfeit gentlemen sporting bogus arms to which they were not entitled. In 1616, Garter King of Arms and York Herald were summoned before the Earl Marshal's commissioners and committed to the Marshalsea for facilitating the granting of arms to one 'Gregory Brandon of London, Gentleman' who, it transpired, was the common hangman of the City of London. The felony was further compounded when it was discovered that Garter, the senior officer of arms, had failed to recognize that Brandon's new coat comprised the combined arms of the sovereigns of Aragon and Brabant! The Lord Chamberlain expressed the wish 'that this their Durance might make the one more Wise, and the other more honest'.

Contemporary society was obsessed with the trappings of rank and, therefore, with matters heraldic. In the first half of the seventeenth century, notions of medieval chivalry were expressed most dogmatically in numerous widely-read treatises on heraldry and 'handbooks' for gentlemen. This preoccupation with form, and with the 'correctness' of society, is reflected in a proliferation of heraldic 'rules' and an almost obsessional concern for the niceties of blazon (the terminology of heraldry). It is also evident in the increasing complexity of marshalling and in the stylized funeral heraldry and monuments of the period (*see* page 96).

The armorial bearings of Sir Francis Drake.
A fine, simple shield with an impossibly complicated crest

Explorers and Swashbucklers

Christopher Columbus (1451–1506) died in poverty and obscurity. But while both his character and achievements have become matters of controversy, the arms granted to him by Ferdinand and Isabella of Spain are singularly unambiguous. Columbus adopted the motto 'To Castile and Leon Columbus gives a new world' and, to acknowledge their gratitude, the king and queen granted quarterings of the allusive gold castle on red of Castile and the red lion on silver of Leon, together with anchors and islands to commemorate Columbus' discoveries.

Encouraged by Elizabeth I, Francis Drake (1540–96) plundered Spanish shipping with impunity and, in 1577, he circumnavigated the globe – an event for which he was knighted. Although he could not prove kinship, Sir Francis assumed the red wyvern arms of the Drake family of Devonshire. But while piracy on the high seas was encouraged, it was not tolerated in heraldic circles and Sir Bernard Drake, the lawful owner of the wyvern arms, boxed Sir Francis' ears and demanded that justice be done. The Queen responded by granting Sir Francis arms 'which he should bear by her special favour': a black shield with a silver wavy *fess* (representing the course of his voyage) between two Pole stars. His crest, which could never have been borne on a helmet, was a ship, drawn round a globe by the hand of God issuing from clouds (*see* page 91). Sir Bernard was not impressed and declared: 'The Queen may have given you finer arms than mine, but she cannot give you the right to bear the wyvern, the cognisance of my house.' Inevitably, Sir Francis had the last word. Entirely without authority, he added a red wyvern to his crest and (on occasions) continued to quarter the arms of the Devonshire Drakes with his own.

Nearly four centuries later another swashbuckler, Douglas Fairbanks Junior, 'America's unofficial ambassador of goodwill' and a knight of the British Empire, was also granted honorary arms which symbolize the two hemispheres united across the blue Atlantic by a golden knot of friendship.

Sir Walter Ralegh (*c.* 1552–1618), explorer, courtier and favourite of the Queen bore *Gules five Fusils conjoined in bend Argent* (some sources suggest seven *fusils*) and it was he who gave his name to the city of Ralegh in Virginia. It is likely that this was the first American corporation to be granted arms (in 1586) and the patent also included grants of personal arms for the Governor, John White, and the twelve Assistants. All these arms contain references to Sir Walter's heraldry in their white and red tinctures and by the inclusion of *fusils* in a variety of combinations.

Christopher Columbus

Sir Walter Ralegh

The arms and crest of Douglas Fairbanks Jnr

North America

In 1705 Laurence Cromp, York Herald, was appointed President of the Court of Honour and Principal Herald of the Province of Carolina with authority to grant arms to 'a certain number of Landgraves and Cassiques, who may be and are the Perpetual and Hereditary Nobles and Peers of our said Province.' There is little evidence to suggest that Carolina Herald took his duties seriously and only two creations are recorded, both of which emanated from the Lords Proprietors of the province.

The American colonies declared themselves independent of Britain on 4 July 1776 at a time when Isaac Heard, a future Garter King of Arms whose wife was a native of Boston, was beginning to establish a regulated heraldic system in the colonies by means of grants of arms and the registration of pedigrees proving a right to arms by descent. There can be little doubt that, but for independence, under Heard's influence North America would have followed British heraldic practice, and it is interesting to note that a number of later English grants, made to men who had left after the Revolution, were extended to include members of a grantee's family in America. To Heard may be attributed many of the complex, often 'landscaped', designs evident in arms and augmentations of the period.

In 1869, John Von Sonnentgan Haviland, an English herald of American birth, gave evidence before an Earl Marshal's inquiry stating that the College of Arms had consistently refused to register the pedigrees of Americans who wished to trace their descent from English families. For most Americans at the beginning of the present century, the only way to obtain a grant of arms was to trace a remote cousin who might be persuaded to petition for a grant with extended limitations to include descendants of a common ancestor. But, at some unrecorded date, the English kings of arms began granting honorary arms to eminent Americans who could prove unbroken male descent from British subjects. There is now a requirement that claims should be confirmed by reference to pedigrees registered at the College of Arms. The English kings of arms have no jurisdiction in the United States but, since 1962, several American corporations have obtained heraldic designs (devisals) from the College of Arms. These are similar in appearance to letters patent and are issued only with the consent of a state governor.

In 1983, the town of Manteo, North Carolina, applied for a devisal of arms. The arms *Argent on a Cross Gules six Lozenges conjoined palewise of the field in dexter chief a Roebuck statant also Gules* are a variation of those granted in the sixteenth century to the city of Ralegh on the site of which Manteo now stands.

Arms of the family of George Washington
1732–99

Assumed arms of Dwight D. Eisenhower
1890–1969

The arms of Sir Isaac Heard:
Left: His alleged ancestral arms
Right: The arms granted to him
in 1774

The town arms of Manteo, North Carolina, 1983

Funeral Accoutrements

Funerals of the late medieval and Tudor nobility were often magnificent spectacles, not least the processions which preceded the committal in which the deceased's heraldic 'achievements' were paraded. These included his spurs, gauntlets, crested helm, shield, sword, tabard and banner which were retained for display in the church, the best-known examples being those of Edward, the Black Prince (d. 1376) at Canterbury Cathedral.

It was said of Thomas Howard, the 2nd Duke of Norfolk, that 'no nobleman was ever to be buried in such style again'. Following his death in May 1524, the Duke's body lay in state for a month in the chapel of Framlingham Castle, Suffolk, in which were hung funereal drapes and numerous shields of arms. The Duke's coffin, drawn on a chariot and embellished with gold shields, was accompanied on its twenty-four mile progress to Thetford Priory in Norfolk by 900 mourners including heralds, gentlemen of his household and numerous black-robed torch-bearers. At Thetford the coffin was placed on an enormous black and gold catafalque, adorned with 700 lights, eight black-robed wax effigies supporting 'ban-nerols', and 100 richly emblazoned shields of arms. The service included a procession of heralds carrying the Duke's arms and the dramatic entry of a mounted knight, wearing the dead Duke's armour and carrying his inverted battle-axe.

Several less grandiose examples of funeral achievements have survived from the sixteenth century and from these may be traced the gradual evolution of funeral heraldry from the practical equipment of medieval warfare and tournament through the stylized, artificial helms, crests and tabards of the late Tudor period to the heraldic substitute, the funeral hatchment, of the seventeenth, eighteenth and nineteenth centuries (*see* page 98). At St Mary Redcliffe, Bristol the monument of Admiral Sir William Penn (d. 1670), whose son founded Pennsylvania, is surmounted and flanked by his breastplate, crested helm, gauntlet, spurs, shield, banner and pennons. But for the most part, only odd items remain. At Swinbrook, Oxfordshire, for example, there are two imitation helms with the griffin crests of the Fettiplace family and at Aldershot, Hampshire stylized funeral helms bear the crests of Sir John White (d. 1573) and his son Richard (d. 1599).

Banners of members of the various orders of knighthood will be found in many British churches. These are invariably 1.5 metres square (5 feet), embroidered with the knight's arms and fringed in two or more colours. The banner of a deceased knight is the perquisite of the king of arms of the order to which he belonged but, in practice, it is normally conveyed to the family and displayed in their parish church.

Typical 19C hatchment – a corruption of the word 'achievement'

One of the eight stone 'weepers' from the tomb of Philippe Pot, Grand Senechal of Burgundy 1493

Heralds in procession at the funeral of Sir Philip Sidney in 1586. Each figure carries a funeral achievement belonging to the deceased

Hatchments

A descendant of the medieval funeral achievement, a hatchment is a diamond-shaped heraldic panel usually found in a church where it may be affixed to a wall or removed to a ringing chamber or some other equally inaccessible quarter. It was carried in a cortège and, following interment, was erected above the door of the deceased's house during a period of mourning before being returned to the church. The use of hatchments was at its peak in the mid nineteenth century but declined rapidly during Victoria's reign.

Hatchments, the earliest of which date from c. 1627, comprise a shield of arms (often with helm, crest and mantling and, where appropriate, a peer's coronet and supporters) painted on a wooden panel or on canvas within a wooden frame.

It is the treatment of the background which makes the hatchment unique: essentially, this is coloured black beneath those parts of a coat of arms which relate to the deceased. Thus, the background of the hatchment to a deceased husband will be black in the dexter half (beneath the late husband's arms) and white in the sinister half (beneath those of the surviving wife) (1). When a wife is an heraldic heiress her arms are correctly shown on a small shield at the centre of her husband's (described as *in pretence*). But because this cannot be reflected in the colour of the background, the arms are sometimes placed side by side (*impaled*) or both impaled and *in pretence* and the appropriate background used. This is contrary to the normal conventions of marshalling (*see* Chapter 8), as are the various methods that may be used to indicate two or more wives in a single hatchment. For this purpose, the sinister half of the shield may be divided with the arms of the first wife at the top and those of the second wife below (9). Alternatively, the shield may be divided vertically into three with the husband's arms in the centre between those of his first wife to the dexter and his second wife's to the sinister (7). This may be confused with another method in which the husband's arms appear in the dexter and those of his former wives successively to the sinister (8). A further (and less confusing) method was to depict the husband's personal arms in the centre and the impaled arms of his various wives on small shields set in panels on either side (10).

Eighteenth- and nineteenth-century illustrations and engravings and the records of antiquarian county histories indicate that there were once many more hatchments in British parish churches than the 4500 recorded in the recent past. Canvas and wood are unlikely to survive centuries of damp and neglect or the over-enthusiastic 'restorations' of the nineteenth century.

HATCHMENTS

1. Husband
   (wife surviving)
2. Wife
   (husband surviving)
3. Bachelor
4. Widow
5. Widower
6. Spinster

7, 8, 9 and 10
   Husband
   (second wife
   surviving)

Heraldry in Wales

Throughout Welsh heraldry there are examples of apparently unrelated families who share the same arms: Llewelyn of Hendrescythen, Williams of Aberpergwym and Thomas of Pwllywrach, for example, all bear *Gules three Chevronels Argent*, as do the families of Avan, Evans of Gnoll, Leyson, Loughor and Pryce of Duffryn.

The reason for this is that Welsh heraldry is fundamentally different in that its purpose is to proclaim ancestry as well as gentility. The majority of the Welsh nation consists of a pedigreed population, a distinct caste, descended from the native Welsh aristocracy of royal, noble and gentle families; the warrior farmers (the 'landed gentry' as they would be known in England); and the *advenae*, the Norman and English feudal lords who held lands in the Welsh Marches – often described as 'adventurers' in Welsh manuscripts.

The ancient social system of the Welsh, in which so many rights and obligations were dependent on membership of a tribe, conditioned them to regard a pedigree as of the utmost importance. In Wales there was no such person as an 'armigerous gentleman' as there was in England, for a man was 'gentle' by virtue of his genealogy and gentility followed the blood: 'For a great temporal blessing it is and a great heart's ease to a man to find that he is well descended' (Sir John Wynn of Gwidir d. 1626).

Although the Welsh had been acquainted with medieval heraldry and many 'native born' magnates had adopted arms, it was not until the early Tudor period, and the visitations of the English heralds, that they produced a system. Those Welshmen who already bore arms were assumed to have inherited them from tribal ancestors while new arms were attributed to the ancestors of other, non-armigerous families. For example, the numerous descendants of Hywel Dda who lived in the tenth century, those of Cadwaladr who lived in the seventh, of Cunedda who lived in the fifth and of Beli Mawr who probably never lived at all, all received retrospective coats of arms which they hurriedly registered with the English heralds of the new Tudor dynasty. Once attributed to an ancient ancestor, the arms could then be borne legitimately by all who could prove descent from him. A Welsh Tudor gentleman tended to quarter the arms of all his ancestors, therefore, his quarterings proclaiming that he was a descendant of a particular ancestor or ancestors and, therefore, a gentleman by blood. For example, all the families who now bear the arms *Gules three Chevronels Argent* claim descent from Iestyn ap Gwrgant, King of Morgannwg, who ruled the territories of what is now Glamorgan in the late eleventh century and from whom descended the lords of Afan, Baglan, Machen, Miskin and Senghenydd.

Arms of some of the royal and noble families of Wales

1. Elystan Glodrudd, King of Rhwng Gwy ag Hafren (11C). 2. Iestyn ap
Gwrgant, King of Morgannwg (11C). 3. Ynyr, King of Gwent (11C). 4. Gweirydd ap
Rhys Goch of Anglesey (12C). 5. Nefydd Hardd of Caernarvonshire (12C).
6. Ednywain ap Bradwen of Merionethshire (12C). 7. Cadifor ap Dinawal (12C).
8. Ifor Hael of Monmouthshire (14C). 9. Llywelyn Crugeryr of Radnorshire (14C)

Scottish Heraldry

The red lion of the Scottish kings was adopted as a device by William I (1165–1214) – known as 'The Lion' – and first appears within a border of *fleurs-de-lis* during the reign of his son, Alexander II (1214–49). In the great seal of Alexander III (1251), this *bordure* was translated into a *double Tressure flory counter flory* and remains today in the royal arms of Scotland. The red lion crest was introduced during the reign of David II (1329–70) and from *c.*1502 was depicted as *sejant* and holding a sword and a flag charged with a St Andrew's cross (a *saltire*), though the latter was subsequently replaced by a gold sceptre. The original supporters were two *lions guardant* – the familiar silver unicorns were introduced in 1440. In 1603, when James VI of Scotland succeeded to the English throne as James I, the royal arms of the two kingdoms were marshalled with the quarterings and supporters transposed in order to reflect sovereignty in either country. (The present royal arms of Scotland are here illustrated and those of the Stuart kings of England are to be found on page 106.)

In the social organization of Scottish society the Clan, the Family and the Name remain as significant entities, revered by all those of Scots descent who wear the crest badge of their chief.

In Scottish heraldry undifferenced arms are borne only by Heads of Clans or Chiefs of a Family or Name. It is an offence to bear arms unless they have been matriculated with Lord Lyon King of Arms and entered into the *Public Register of All Arms and Bearings in Scotland*. Matriculation is not simply registration; the process requires the correct marshalling of the arms, together with appropriate amendments (*brisures*) indicating relationships within an armigerous family. Armorial bearings are succeeded to by the heir who uses a *label* which, as in England, is eventually discarded. Cadets, the younger sons of an armiger and progenitors of subsidiary branches of a family, are assigned amended versions of their paternal arms when they matriculate with Lord Lyon. These descend to their children on matriculation, again with appropriate differences (*see* Chapter 8).

In Scotland all matters heraldic are the sole responsibility of Lord Lyon King of Arms and all decisions are in his prerogative, acting on behalf of the Sovereign. In this he is assisted by a number of officers of arms whose titles vary from time to time but currently include Marchmont, Albany and Rothesay heralds and Dingwall, Kintyre, Carrick and Unicorn pursuivants. In Scotland there are also several 'private' officers of arms: Slains and Garioch heralds, for example, who serve the Earl of Erroll and the Countess of Mar respectively.

IN DEFENS

NEMO ME LACESSIT

IMPUNE

The royal arms of Scotland

The royal badges of
Scotland. *Left:* The Crowned
Thistle. *Right:* The Regal
Saltire – a silver saltire
enfiling a gold open crown

Irish Heraldry

There are three heraldic traditions relating to the arms of Ireland. The first of these was the Anglo-Irish medieval tradition by which the arms *Azure three Crowns Gold* came to be associated with the medieval lordship of Ireland. These were the attributed arms of St Edmund the Martyr (*see* page 14), a favourite saint of the Norman barons of Ireland and of the Irish magnates recruited by Edward I to fight in the Scottish wars of 1296–1307. In 1386, Richard II granted the arms of the lordship (within a silver border) as an augmentation to Robert de Vere on his creation as Marquis of Dublin and (shortly thereafter) Duke of Ireland. In 1467–8 a commission of Edward IV determined that the three gold crowns on blue were indeed the ancient arms of Ireland and thereafter they were widely used on coins and seals, though from 1533 as the arms of the medieval lordship rather than those of the kingdom.

The second tradition provided the now familiar *Azure a Harp Gold stringed Argent* – the legendary Harp of Tara adopted by Henry VIII as a royal device together with the title *Hibernie Rex*: King of Ireland. These arms first appeared in the Wijnbergen Roll, a French armorial of *c.*1280–1330 in which they may have referred to the legendary 'le roi d'Irelande' of the Tristan cycle. They later appear in the Rous Roll of 1483–4, as one of the crests of Richard III's dominions, were confirmed as the arms of the Kingdom of Ireland in *c.*1547 and, on the accession of the Stuarts in 1603, were quartered with the arms of England and Scotland where they have remained ever since.

In Eire today the arms of the four provinces are popularly quartered as the arms of Ireland: Leinster (*Vert a Harp Gold*), Connacht (*Per pale Argent and Azure* in the first *an Eagle dimidiated and displayed Sable* in the second *an Arm embowed and vested the Hand holding a Sword erect all Argent*), Ulster (*Gold on a Cross Gules an Inescutcheon Argent charged with a dexter Hand erect Gules*) and Munster (*Azure three Antique Crowns Gold*). They are also to be found in the arms of the Genealogical Office where they are quartered beneath a *Chief Gules charged with a Portcullis Or between two Scrolls Argent*.

Since 1943, the Chief Herald of Ireland has exercised heraldic and genealogical authority within the Republic from the Genealogical Office in Kildare Street, Dublin. He grants arms only to persons of Irish descent who may be considered to have reached 'the port of gentry'. Heraldic jurisdiction over the province of Northern Ireland is vested in the office of Norroy and Ulster King of Arms in London.

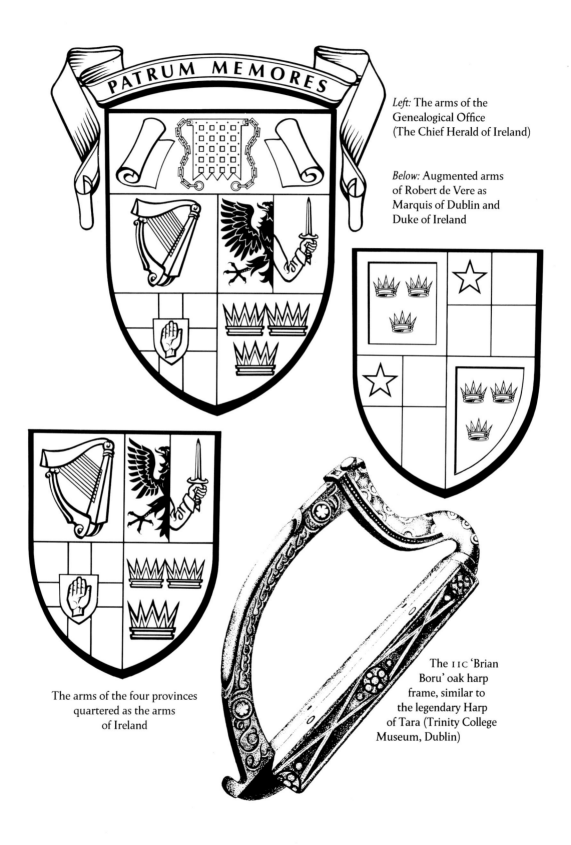

PATRUM MEMORES

Left: The arms of the
Genealogical Office
(The Chief Herald of Ireland)

Below: Augmented arms
of Robert de Vere as
Marquis of Dublin and
Duke of Ireland

The arms of the four provinces
quartered as the arms
of Ireland

The 11c 'Brian
Boru' oak harp
frame, similar to
the legendary Harp
of Tara (Trinity College
Museum, Dublin)

Two Stuart devices
symbolizing the union
of England and Scotland

The royal arms of Stuart

5   From Stuart to Windsor

When, in 1603, James VI of Scotland succeeded to the English throne as James I, the arms of the two kingdoms were combined by means of grand quartering with the sub-quarters of France and England in the first and third grand-quarters, Scotland in the second and Ireland in the third. The English crest and motto were retained and the dragon supporter of the Tudors was replaced by a Scottish unicorn.

But the new royal arms were not arrived at without contention. The Irish harp, which had hitherto been borne separately and only for Irish purposes, was included for the first time as the third quartering (where, at times incongruously, it has remained ever since). But there was an often acrimonious debate with regard to the precedence of the English and Scottish quarterings and supporters: 'Like as a Lyon, whose imperiall powre / A prowd rebellious Unicorn defyes ...' (Spencer). The Scots argued that James's paternal arms were those of Scotland and it was Scotland that had added England to her dominions and not the other way round. Therefore, according to heraldic convention, the Scottish arms should be borne in the first quarter and the unicorn supporter should occupy the senior dexter position. But clearly this would not be acceptable to the English who considered themselves to be the senior partner in the European hierarchy.

The problem was resolved by creating two coats of arms: one for the King of England and the other for the King of Scots. As king of Scotland, James and his successors reversed the quarterings, so that the arms of Scotland were given precedence in the first and fourth quarters with England/France in the second and Ireland in the third. Similarly, the supporters 'changed sides' and the Scottish crest and mottoes were retained. This heraldic distinction between the two kingdoms is still observed.

Just as Henry VII had combined the red and white roses of Lancaster and York in the Tudor Rose, so James I brought together the Scottish thistle and English rose in a device that symbolized the coming together of the two kingdoms – either dimidiated (half rose and half thistle) or both springing from a common stalk.

The Union Flag

The design proposed for the Union Jack of 1606 was equally controversial. This was to be a combination of the saltire of St Andrew and the St George's cross: national badges that for centuries had been used on standards and uniforms to identify the nationality of military contingents (*see* page 60).

As the name 'jack' suggests, the flag was intended for naval purposes. Medieval and Tudor naval commanders used their personal arms on banners and sails together with streamers which, like military standards, bore their badges on a background of livery colours. National devices were also flown and, in the Elizabethan period, these included a variety of striped ensigns, some of which incorporated the cross of St George.

The 1606 design placed the English cross over the Scottish saltire, thereby giving it precedence. This arrangement inevitably invited hostility from the Scots and there is evidence that, through the seventeenth and eighteenth centuries, a 'Scotch Union Flag' was sometimes used in which the St Andrew's saltire was placed on top of the St George's cross.

The Union Jack was originally intended for general use at sea but in 1634 Charles I restricted its use to ships of the 'Navie Royall' and proclaimed that, in future, privately owned English and Scottish ships were to revert to flying their national flags. Correctly, it should be termed the Union Flag, a jack being a small version, of rather square proportions, flown from a jack staff at the bowsprit.

In 1707, the Act of Union of the Two Kingdoms of England and Scotland included a clause which stated 'that ... the Crosses of St George and St Andrew be cojoined in such manner as Her Majesty shall think fit' and the earlier design was confirmed.

At the union with Ireland in 1801 the red 'St Patrick' saltire on white of the FitzGeralds was placed over the Scottish saltire. But the Scots, who had never wholly been reconciled to the precedence given to the English cross, objected angrily that their saltire was all but obliterated by that of Ireland. The matter was resolved by dividing the Scottish and Irish saltires, placing the two halves side by side and providing the latter with a narrow white border (*fimbriation*) so that the broad white stripe of Scotland appears above the narrow Irish one when the flag is hoisted, thereby confirming the seniority of the Scottish device.

The complex blazon of the Union Flag is: *Azure the Crosses Saltire of St Andrew and St Patrick quarterly per saltire counterchanged Argent and Gules the latter fimbriated of the second surmounted by the Cross of St George of the third fimbriated as the Saltire.*

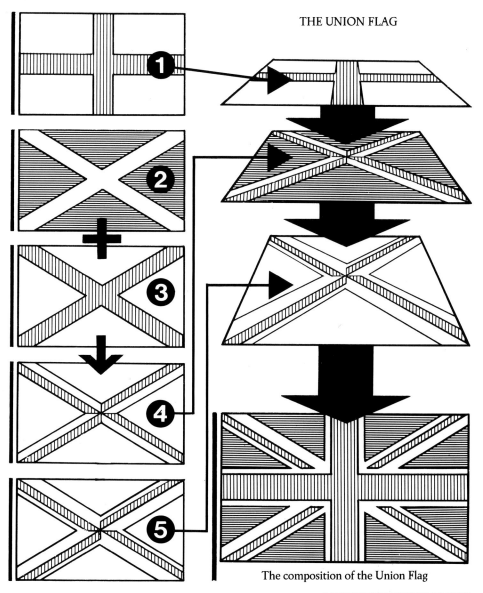

The composition of the Union Flag

1. Cross of St George
2. Saltire of St Andrew
3. Saltire of St Patrick
4. Saltires combined and counterchanged
5. St Patrick saltire fimbriated

The Union Flag of 1707

The Commonwealth

With the execution of Charles I and the establishment of the Common-wealth in 1649, kingship was declared to be 'unnecessary, burdensome and dangerous to the liberty, safety and public interest of the people'. In many places (notably in parish churches) the royal arms were destroyed or defaced while others were taken down and hidden or turned round and the Commonwealth arms painted on the reverse.

But the heraldry of the Commonwealth (1649–60) suggests that Oliver Cromwell (Lord Protector 1653–8) either entertained monarchal aspirations or that he acknowledged the transitory nature of the republic and recognized that he held the monarchy in trust. Having refused the crown, he nevertheless incorporated the symbols of sovereignty in the arms of the Commonwealth that appeared on the Great Seal of 1655. The royal helm, crown, crest and supporter of a crowned lion were all retained, while the shield (*Quarterly 1 and 4 Argent a Cross Gules* [for England] *2 Azure a Saltire Argent* [for Scotland] *and 3 Azure a Harp Or stringed Argent* [for Ireland] also included an inescutcheon of the arms of Cromwell himself (*Sable a Lion rampant Argent*). Significantly, the Scottish unicorn supporter, with its Stuart associations, was replaced by the Welsh dragon and, according to Sir Bernard Burke, when Cromwell's coffin was opened it was found to contain a copper plate engraved with the royal arms of England impaling his own.

In 1649, Parliament ordered gold and silver coins to be struck with English inscriptions instead of Latin and no portraits. On the obverse of the larger coins was a shield of the cross of St George within a laurel wreath and the legend *THE COMMONWEALTH AND ENGLAND*. On the reverse, the shields of St George and the harp of Ireland were depicted side by side, with the words *GOD WITH US*. Protector Cromwell intended to mint a very fine set of new coins but few seem to have been circulated. Again, these incorporated the royal crown together with Cromwell's personal arms which were depicted at the centre of a shield comprising the crosses of St George and St Andrew and the Irish harp.

Following the restoration of Charles II in 1660, a statute requiring that the royal arms should be displayed in all churches resulted in many old boards being brought out of hiding and re-painted or new ones made. Wherever the Commonwealth arms were displayed they were to 'be forthwith taken down; and that the King's Majesty's Arms be set up instead thereof'. On 11 May 1660, Pepys records: 'This morning we began to pull down all the State's arms in the fleet, having first sent to Dover for painters and others to come to set up the King's.'

The arms of the Commonwealth

Below: The arms of Oliver Cromwell

Augmentations of Honour

A coat of arms may be augmented by means of an additional charge or alteration granted in recognition of signal service to the Crown and as such is held in great esteem.

Many of these honourable augmentations date from the English civil war when, in 1645, Charles I empowered Garter King of Arms to make special awards to valiant royalists. One such grant was that to Dr Edward Lake who was granted a quartering of honour which included sixteen escutcheons (small shields), said to represent the sixteen wounds the doctor received at the battle of Edgehill. For a crest, he was granted a representation of himself on horseback, spattered with blood and holding the bridle in his teeth. The arms of the city of Hereford were augmented with a blue border charged with ten silver saltires of St Andrew: 'for there hath not any city ... expressed greater fidelity and courage ... when, being straitly besieged for a space of five weeks by a powerful army of rebellious Scots, they ... defended themselves ... with so great destruction of the besiegers that they became the wonder of the neighbouring garrisons ... and do justly deserve such characters of honour.' The augmentation clearly represents the City besieged by the 'army of rebellious Scots'.

There are numerous augmentations dating from the Restoration, granted to royalists when 'the King enjoyed his own again' in 1660, and these record Charles's escapades as well as any historical novel. A red shield with a crowned, golden portcullis was added to the arms of Colonel Newman who assisted in Charles's escape from Worcester in 1651. The famous 'Royal Oak', in which Charles hid 'While underneath the Round-head rode', is commemorated in the arms of Colonel Careless who shared the Prince's refuge and whose inappropriate name the King later changed to Carlos; while identical arms (though of different tinctures) were granted to the Penderel family of Boscobel on whose land the oak tree stood and who provided the Prince with shelter and clothing. A red rose within a wreath of oak leaves was granted to the family of Whitgreave who, threatened by Parliamentary troops, stubbornly refused to reveal Charles's presence in their house at Moseley. Even more remarkable is the *Canton of England* granted to the Lane family after Mistress Jane Lane courageously allowed herself to be 'escorted' by the Prince, disguised as her servant, to Bristol from where he hoped to embark for France. The strawberry roan on which he rode is commemorated in the Lane crest.

Charles finally set sail from Shoreham in Sussex in a ship commissioned by one Francis Mansell of Guildford whose arms of *Or three Maunches Sable* (stylized sleeves) were augmented with a *Lion of England*, together with a crest of a ship with three crowns on the stern and flying the St George's cross.

AUGMENTATIONS of HONOUR

Mansell crest

Lane crest

1

2

3

4

5

6

7

1. City of Hereford
   Besieged by the Scots
2. Mansell
   Charles' escape to France
3. Lane
   Prince's ride to Bristol
4. Newman
   The flight from Worcester
5. Lake
   Battle of Edgehill
6. Whitegreave
   The fugitive's concealment
7. Carlos
   The oak-tree incident

The Peerage

In the Middle Ages, the term 'lord' was synonymous with 'sire' and implied feudal superiority. It is now used as the abbreviated style of a peer below the rank of duke and as an honorary prefix used by the younger sons of dukes and marquesses. It is also the style of Scottish Lords of Sessions.

The term 'peerage' includes the British degree of duke, marquess, earl, viscount and baron, all of which are hereditary. Derived from the medieval Latin *paragium*, it means simply 'a company of equals' and was originally applied to those of similar rank within the nobility. From 1321, the term was used to describe those senior barons of England who normally received writs of summons to Parliament and, later, to the lords spiritual. The British peerage now comprises five separate peerages: those of England, Scotland, Ireland, Great Britain and the United Kingdom. The peerages of England and Scotland were combined at the Act of Union in 1707 as the Peerage of Great Britain, and the Peerage of Ireland continued until 1801 when a further Act of Union created the Peerage of the United Kingdom, though occasional creations continued after that date. In their coats of arms, peers use a silver helmet with gold bars, a coronet appropriate to their rank (*see* also page 158) and supporters. The coronation robes of peers are of crimson velvet, edged with miniver, the cape furred with miniver and embellished with rows of ermine: four rows for dukes, three rows and a half for marquesses, three for earls, two and a half for viscounts and two for barons. Parliamentary robes are of fine scarlet cloth, lined with taffeta and embellished with bands (guards) of fur: four guards of ermine with gold lace above each guard for dukes, four on the right side and three on the left for marquesses, three for earls, and two guards of plain white fur for both viscounts and barons.

A dukedom is the senior rank of the British peerage. Derived from the Latin *dux*, meaning 'leader', the rank was introduced into England in 1337 although the style had been known before that date, William the Conqueror being referred to as *Ducis Normannorum et Regis Anglorum*, for example. The first English non-royal dukedom was granted to Henry, Earl of Lancaster, Derby, Lincoln and Leicester in 1351 while in Scotland, David, the eldest son of Robert III, became Duke of Rothesay in 1398. The wife of a duke is a duchess.

A marquess (or marquis) belongs to the second rank of the British peerage. Although introduced from Europe in 1385, the term *marchiones* had previously been used by lords of the Welsh and Scottish marches. The wife of a marquess is a marchioness.

Duke

Silver-gilt coronet of eight strawberry leaves (three and two halves visible) with crimson velvet cap. Mantle has four rows of ermine on the cape

Marquess

Coronet of silver gilt with four strawberry leaves (one and two halves visible) and four silver balls (two visible). Mantle has three rows and a half of ermine on the cape

Earl

Coronet has eight silver balls raised upon points (five visible) and alternate gold strawberry leaves. The mantle has a cape with three rows of ermine

Several of the lords who followed Duke William in his conquest of England held substantial territories (*comtés*) in the Low Countries and France and, although granted English lands and titles by the Conqueror, they retained the superior title of *comté*, *county* or count. The English equivalent of count is earl, a title which originated in Scandinavia and appeared in England in the early eleventh century as *eorl*, an Old English form of *jarl*. Prior to 1337, when the Black Prince was created a duke, it was the senior rank of the nobility. The earliest known charter creating an hereditary earl is that of *c*.1140 by which King Stephen created Geoffrey de Mandeville Earl of Essex. An earldom is now the third rank of the British peerage and the wife of an earl (or one who holds an earldom in her own right) is a countess.

A viscount belongs to the fourth rank of the British peerage, the first creation being of 1440, though the title itself is considerably older. In the days of the Carolingian empire the *vice-comtés* were the deputies of the counts and gradually assumed hereditary rights. The wife of a viscount is a viscountess.

The word 'baron' is of uncertain origin. It was introduced into England following the Norman Conquest of 1066 to identify the 'man' (vassal) of a great lord, though prior to the Conquest a *barony* was simply a chief's domain. In Ireland a *barony* was a medieval division of a county, corresponding to the English hundred. Following the Conquest, tenants-in-chief of the king below the rank of earl were often referred to as barons, and from the thirteenth century the title appears to have been reserved for those magnates summoned by writ to parliament: greater barons being those who were summoned by direct writ to the king's council and lesser barons were those summoned through the county sheriffs. During the reign of Edward IV (1461–83) a new and powerful merchant class emerged (principally as a result of Edward's encouragement of trade and commerce) and this was to bring about the eventual dissolution of the feudal baronage. The style itself was introduced by Richard II in 1387 and it is now the fifth and lowest rank of the British peerage. The Life Peerage Act of 1958 enabled the Crown to create non-hereditary peerages with the rank and style of baron.

In Scotland, the equivalent rank is that of a Lord in Parliament while the Baronage of Scotland is a feudal institution entirely different from the English baronage and of similar status to an English lord of the manor.

Viscount

Silver-gilt coronet
with sixteen silver
balls (nine visible).
Mantle has a cape
with two rows and a
half of ermine

Baron

A plain silver-gilt
circlet set with six
silver balls (four
visible). Mantle has
two rows of ermine
on the cape

In a peer's letters patent of creation, the ceremonial insignia include 'a Cap of Honour' worn with 'a Coronet of Gold' on occasions of state. These coronets of rank are the lineal descendants of the combined medieval chapeau and gold circlet which, in the fourteenth century, were restricted to dukes and marquesses and, after 1444, also to earls, though at that time they do not appear to have conformed to any particular pattern. Coronets were first granted to viscounts by James I and to barons by Charles II in 1661.

Baronets and Knights

A baronetcy is an hereditary rank of the British peerage. Created by James I in 1611, with the objective of raising money to support his troops in Ulster, the first recipients paid £1095 for the style Sir and Lady (or Dame) and precedence above knights. In 1625 a baronetage of Scotland was established, to provide funds for the colonization of Nova Scotia, and both creations lasted until 1707 when they were replaced by the baronetage of Great Britain. In 1619 the baronetage of Ireland was created and, on 1st January 1801, both the baronetage of Great Britain and that of Ireland were replaced by the baronetage of the United Kingdom which continues to the present day.

Baronets of England, Ireland, Great Britain and the United Kingdom have as their badge 'the bloody hand of Ulster' – a red hand on a white shield or *canton* – borne as an augmentation in their arms. Baronets of Scotland wear a badge comprising the shield of arms of Nova Scotia within a blue circlet and this is depicted, suspended from a tawny coloured ribbon, beneath the shield. All baronets are entitled to use a knight's helmet in their arms, this being of steel, full-faced and with the visor raised (*see* pages 154–5).

The word 'knighthood' is the modern form of the Old English *cnihthád*, the period between youth and maturity, while the word 'chivalry' is derived from the Old French *chevalerie* meaning 'armed horsemen'. By the mid twelfth century the two words were virtually synonymous and described both the personal attributes and the code of conduct of the mounted warrior.

The sons of the medieval nobility were schooled in the arts of war and chivalry as members of the households of their fathers' peers. They were expected to progress through the degrees of page, esquire, knight bachelor and (for some) knight banneret.

The banneret was originally a chief feudal tenant or lesser baron whose rank was between that of knight bachelor and baron. In the Middle Ages, a banneret was permitted to lead troops in battle under his own banner which, because it was of smaller dimensions than those of his superiors, was also termed a 'banneret' (*see* page 42).

Knights Bachelor belong to the lowest degree of knighthood but also the most ancient. Knights were originally required to perform military service (knight's fee) in exchange for granted lands but this duty was gradually commuted to a money payment known as 'shield money' (*scutage*). A knight bachelor was not a member of an order of chivalry and, in the medieval army, he would command the smallest unit, perhaps consisting of only a few personal retainers.

Badge of the
Knight Bachelor

Baronet of the United Kingdom

Baronet of Nova Scotia

Shields of arms of three baronets of the United Kingdom
in which the badge augments the original arms

Plender
of Ovenden

Blunt
of Lamberhurst

Isham
of Lamport

Orders of Chivalry

Mention has already been made (on page 36) of the foundation, in 1348, of the Order of the Garter: the oldest and most prestigious order of chivalry in Britain. The original fellowship consisted of the sovereign and his eldest son together with twenty-four young men of noble birth. In 1786 membership was extended to the lineal descendants of George III, even though the chapter might be complete, and again in 1805 and 1831 to include the descendants of George II and George I respectively. Queens of England were, of course, members as Head of the order but it was not until the reign of Edward VII (1901–10) that the King's consort was automatically a 'Lady of the Garter'. In 1987, the statutes of the order were amended so that women could be admitted.

The arms of the order are a red cross on a white ground (*Argent a Cross Gules*), a device attributed to St George, the order's patron saint, and are usually depicted within a Garter. The Garter itself is worn below the left knee or, by ladies, on the left arm. Originally it was light blue but was changed to dark blue in 1714 and is edged, buckled and adorned in gold with the enigmatic motto HONI SOIT QUI MAL Y PENSE ('shame on him who thinks evil of it').

Henry VII introduced the magnificent collar of the order which was composed of twenty-six miniature garters, each encircling a red enamelled rose (originally, Tudor roses), alternating with interlaced knots: 'and at the end of the said collar shall be … fastened The Image of Saint George'. The knights wore a dark blue mantle, on the shoulder of which was embroidered the order's arms, and Charles II introduced a broad blue riband, worn over the left shoulder with a small St George device in plain gold (the 'Lesser George') as a clasp on the right hip. For ceremonial purposes the Knights Companion now wear a dark blue velvet mantle, lined with white taffeta, with the Star of the order on the left breast. The mantle is worn with a crimson velvet hood, lined with white taffeta, and a black velvet hat with an ostrich feather plume and tuft of black heron's feathers affixed with a diamond-studded band.

Knights are entitled to add supporters to their arms and, from the fourteenth century, the most common practice has been to encircle the shield of arms with a representation of the blue and gold Garter inscribed with the motto.

The 1522 statutes of the order require that every Knight Companion shall display his banner, sword, helm and crest above his stall in the order's chapel of St George in Windsor Castle.

The Insignia of the Order of the Garter, c. 1850
1. The Star. 2. Collar and George. 3. Garter. 4. Oval or Lesser George

Banner of Viscount Grey of Falloden KG

Arms of Edward III within the Garter

Banner of the Earl of Harewood KG

The Most Ancient and Most Noble Order of the Thistle was 'revived' in 1687 by James VII of Scotland (James II of England) who asserted that it had been founded by King Achaius in *c*.800. He designed a sumptuous mantle of green velvet powdered with over 250 gold thistles for himself and the twelve knights, a number selected 'in allusion to the Saviour and His Twelve Apostles'. But only eight were appointed before James fled the country in 1688 and the order fell into desuetude. It was revived by Queen Anne in 1703 though the number of member knights remained at eight until a full complement was appointed in 1827. Today the Thistle comprises sixteen Knights Companion in addition to the Sovereign and foreign royalty, and the chapel of the order, at St Giles Kirk in Edinburgh, was dedicated in 1911. Knights are entitled to supporters and to encircle their arms with the collar, circlet and motto of the order and to suspend the badge beneath their arms (*see* page 103). The badge consists of the figure of St Andrew in gold, his gown green and his surcoat purple, bearing before him a white St Andrew's cross (*saltire*), the whole surrounded by golden rays. The motto of the order is NEMO ME IMPUNE LACESSIT ('no one invokes me with impunity').

The motto of the Most Illustrious Order of St Patrick is QUIS SEPARABIT, MDCCLXXXIII – 'Who will sever us, 1783' – a reference to the political considerations which led to its institution by George III in 1783. Although revised in 1905 no appointments have been made since 1934. The order consisted of the Sovereign, Grand Master, twenty-two knights and an additional number of honorary knights, all of whom were entitled to supporters in their arms, to encircle their shields with the collar, circlet and motto of the order and to suspend the insignia beneath the shield. There was no chapel of the order but, before the disestablishment of the Church of Ireland, investitures were normally held in St Patrick's Cathedral, Dublin and, afterwards, in Dublin Castle. The banners and stall plates of former knights remain on display in both buildings.

THE MOST ANCIENT AND MOST NOBLE
ORDER OF THE THISTLE

Breast star and
sash badge

THE MOST ILLUSTRIOUS
ORDER OF ST PATRICK

Breast star and sash badge

The Most Honourable Order of the Bath, the premier meritorious order of the Crown, was established by George IV in 1725. It was modelled on a 'degree of knighthood, which hath been denominated the Knighthood of the Bath' by Henry IV in 1399, the designation acknowledging the ritualistic purification undertaken by a knight-elect prior to his receiving the accolade. In 1735 this degree of knighthood was restored as a 'regular military order' of thirty-six Knights Companion, called the Most Honorary Military Order of the Bath, and Henry VII's chapel in the abbey of Westminster was appointed the chapel of the order. In 1815 the order was reorganized with civil and military divisions and three classes: Knight Grand Cross, Knight Commander and Companion. Knights Grand Cross may add supporters to their arms, the shield of which may be depicted within the circlet of the order inscribed with the motto TRIA JUNCTA IN UNO ('three joined in one').

The Most Distinguished Order of St Michael and St George was founded in 1818 by George III and has subsequently become an honour for British subjects serving overseas, notably in the diplomatic service. There are three classes of membership: Knight and Dame Grand Cross, Knight and Dame Commander and Companion. All may suspend the insignia of the order beneath their arms and surround the shield with the circlet and motto of the order: AUSPICIUM MELIORIS AEVI ('token of a better age') and members of the first class are entitled to supporters. The chapel of the order is in St Paul's Cathedral, London.

The Royal Victorian Order was instituted by Queen Victoria in 1896. There are five classes: Knight and Dame Grand Cross, Knight and Dame Commander, Commander, Lieutenant and Member. Knights and Dames Grand Cross are entitled to supporters and may place the collar of the order around their arms. All classes may suspend the insignia of the order beneath their arms and the first three classes may display their shields within a circlet of the order on which is inscribed the motto VICTORIA. The Chapel of the Savoy is the chapel of the order.

The Most Excellent Order of the British Empire was instituted in 1917, its chapel being in the crypt of St Paul's Cathedral, London. There are military and civil divisions and five classes of membership: Knight Grand Cross, Knight Commander, Commander, Officer and Member. All classes may suspend the appropriate insignia beneath their arms and the first three classes may depict their shields of arms within the circlet of the order on which is inscribed the motto FOR GOD AND THE EMPIRE. Knights Grand Cross are entitled to supporters and may place their shield of arms within the collar of the order.

ORDER OF THE BATH

Star of a
Knight Grand
Cross

Neck badge
(Civil Division)

ORDER OF ST MICHAEL
AND ST GEORGE

Star of a Knight
Grand Cross

Neck badge

Right: ORDER OF THE
BRITISH EMPIRE.
Neck badge

Far right: ROYAL
VICTORIAN ORDER.
Sash badge

The Royal Arms

As Prince of Orange, William III (1689–1702) was entitled to display a number of foreign quarterings together with those of his uncle and father-in-law, James II. But he chose instead to place a simple *inescutcheon* of his paternal arms of Nassau (*Azure billety a Lion rampant Gold*) at the centre of the Stuart arms. Mary II bore the undifferenced arms of the Stuarts (*see* page 106) and there are rare examples of the impaled arms of William and Mary in which the Stuart arms therefore appear side by side.

When William died without issue the crown passed to Mary's sister Anne (1702–14) and, for the first five years of her reign, she bore the arms of Stuart. But, following the Act of Union in 1707, the arms of England and Scotland were impaled in the first and fourth quarters, with the French arms in the second and those of Ireland in the third.

On Anne's death, she was succeeded by George, Elector of Hanover, Duke of Brunswick and Luneberg and Arch Treasurer of the Holy Roman Empire (George I, 1714–27). The fourth quarter was divided into three to accommodate the arms of Brunswick (two gold lions on red), Luneberg (red hearts and a blue *lion rampant* on gold) and Westphalia (a white horse on red) and Charlemagne's crown, on a red shield, was placed at the centre. The royal arms continued in this form during the reigns of George II (1727–60) and George III (1760–1820) until, following the Irish rebellion of 1798, the United Kingdom of Great Britain and Ireland came into being. In 1801, the archaic French arms were omitted and replaced by those of Scotland so that the Irish harp enjoyed equal status with the arms of England and Scotland. The German arms were placed in the centre of the shield together with the Electoral Bonnet which, in 1816, was replaced by a royal crown to signify the translation of the electorate into a kingdom following the Congress of Vienna.

George IV (1820–30) and William IV (1830–37) succeeded to both the British and German possessions and therefore continued to use the arms of their predecessor. But on the death of William IV, Salic Law (which, in Germany, excluded females from dynastic succession) prevented the crown of Hanover passing to a woman and the kingdoms were divided between William's brother, Ernest Augustus, Duke of Cumberland, and his niece, Victoria.

As a consequence, Queen Victoria (1837–1901) removed the shield and crown from the centre of the arms leaving the lions of England in the first and fourth quarters, the lion and *tressure* of Scotland in the second and the Irish harp in the third. These royal arms have been borne by her successors, together with the royal crest and supporters which have remained unchanged from 1603 to the present day.

THE ROYAL ARMS

1689 — 1702

1707 — 1714

1714 — 1801

1801 — 1816

1816 — 1837

1837 —

William III
to
Elizabeth II

Valour and Ostentation

Sir Winston Churchill, Captain of Horse to Charles I, was granted an augmentation of the St George's Cross on a *canton* which he added to his arms *Sable a Lion rampant Argent*. Sir Winston's son, John (1650–1722), was created first Duke of Marlborough by Queen Anne in recognition of his victories over the French forces of Louis XIV, and was granted a further augmentation of a shield of the cross of St George surmounted by the arms of France. Sir Winston Churchill (1874–1965) also bore these augmented arms quartered with those of Spencer (*Quarterly Argent and Gules a Fret Or over all a Bend Sable charged with three Escallops Argent*).

Several eminent British seamen were similarly honoured: Sir Cloudesley Shovel, for example, was granted arms in which silver crescents and a gold *fleur-de-lis* on a red field commemorate his victories over the Franco–Turkish fleet in 1692.

Until the eighteenth century most augmentations of honour were fairly restrained, but a general decline in armorial taste is reflected in several singularly ostentatious augmentations of the period.

Perhaps the best-known example is that of Horatio Nelson, Viscount Nelson and Duke of Bronté (1758–1805) who was first granted an augmentation of a red and gold *bend* charged with three exploding bombs. After the Battle of the Nile he received a further augmentation of a broad wavy line (*a Chief undy*) at the top of his shield, to represent the sea, on which was depicted a landscape with palm tree, disabled ship and a battery in ruins! After Nelson's death a third augmentation was added comprising a *Fess wavy Azure charged with the word 'Trafalgar'*. Of course, all this almost obliterated the original, and beautifully simple, arms of a black cross *patonce* on a gold field.

A further example is to be found in the arms of Lord Harris whose ancestors bore a simple punning shield of three hedgehogs (*herissons*) (*see* page 24). Following the defeat of Tipu Sultan of Mysore (1749–99), the Harris arms were augmented with a crenellated *chevron* bearing three hand grenades and a *chief* charged with *a representation of the sally ports of the capital and fortress of Seringapatam, the drawbridge let down, and the Union Flag of Great Britain and Ireland hoisted over the standard of Tippoo Sultan*. The proud but unfortunate Lord Harris suffered further heraldic indignities: his crest was replaced by Tipu Sultan's crowned tiger, pierced by an arrow and *charged on the forehead with the Persian character for 'Hydery'*, and he was granted supporters of a grenadier and a sepoy bearing respectively the Union Flag and that of the East India Company, hoisted above Tipu Sultan's standard and the French tricolour.

DEO PATRIÆ AMICIS

PLATE 10 **Funeral Hatchment**
The black background beneath the *dexter* dimidiation indicated that
the husband predeceased his wife. 'In Cœlo Quies' is not the family
motto but an aphorism meaning 'Rest in Heaven'.

Previous page: PLATE 9 Arms of Reginald Charles Edward Abbot,
third and last Baron Colchester. The barony became extinct in 1919.

PLATE 11 **Funeral Hatchment**
The black background beneath the *dexter* impalement indicates that
the husband predeceased his wife. 'Resurgam' is not the family
motto but an aphorism meaning 'I shall rise again'.

Overleaf: PLATES 12 & 13 Banners and Supporters

Petre

Antrobus

Walsh

Waldegrave

Pollock

Paulet

Vaughan

Noel

1

2

3

4

5

6

7

8

PLATE 14   **North America**

1. Cook of Toronto
2. Colas of Montreal
3. Bird of Duncan, British Columbia
4. Henwood of Oakwood, Ontario
5. Bowyer of Pain Court, Ontario
6. Ockwell of Calgary, Alberta
7. Beatty of Ottawa
8. Davies of Toronto
9. Johnson of Montgomery, Alabama
10. McCune of Yorba Linda, California
11. Gringras of Montreal
12. Ward of Salt Lake City, Utah

9

10

11

12

1

2

3

4

5

6

7

8

9

10

11

12

PLATE 15 **The United Kingdom**

1. Lancaster of Cheltenham
2. Lovell of Wollaston, Northamptonshire
3. Wood of Over Stratton, Somerset
4. Allen of Henley-on-Thames, Oxon
5. Greenhill of Bournemouth, Dorset
6. Campbell-Kease of Hazelbury Bryan, Dorset
7. Slater of Warminster, Wiltshire
8. Friar of Folke, Dorset
9. Messer of Bath, Avon
10. Herbert of Hackney
11. Holyoake of Hornchurch, Essex
12. Taylor of Pinner, Middlesex

PLATE 16   English letters patent granting a coat of arms and badge to William Huxley of Brisbane, Australia. The arms, which (contrary to the medieval practice) are repeated in the hoist of the standard, are blazoned *Vert gutty d'eau three Chevronels braced each terminating in a Fleur-de-lis Argent*. The badge, which is exemplified beneath the arms, is blazoned *Between the Horns of a Crescent Argent a Sprig of two Gum Nuts of the Spotted Gum Tree (Eucalyptus maculata) Gold*, and the crest includes *A Ground Parrot (Pezoporus wallicus) proper*. Such complex blazons are common in Commonwealth heraldry, though visually the charges are often simple and attractive. In the right-hand margin are the arms of the granting Kings of Arms (Garter, Clarenceux and Norroy and Ulster) whose seals are appended to the document. In England and Wales, letters patent (other than those to bodies corporate) are sealed by Garter and the King of Arms in whose province the armiger resides. Above the text are the arms of the Earl Marshal (the Duke of Norfolk), the Sovereign and the College of Arms. *(Reproduced by kind permission of William Huxley Esq.)*

Augmentations

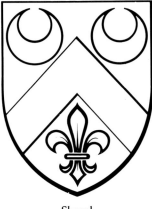

St George's cross on a canton.
First Churchill augmentation

Shovel

Nelson

Banner of Sir Winston Churchill
1874–1965

Civic and Corporate Heraldry

Civic heraldry in Britain dates from the late twelfth century when officials of boroughs and other towns made use of seals carrying devices. Initially, these were rarely depicted on shields and were simply religious or other emblems of local significance, or seigniorial devices indicative of feudal allegiance or benefaction, contained within an inscribed border.

With the gradual development of corporate authority in the Middle Ages came a corresponding desire to assert corporate identity in a form which could be equated with that of the feudal magnate, and by the fourteenth century many towns, guilds and corporations had adopted the devices of their seals as coats of arms. The first recorded grant of arms to a corporate body was that to the Draper's Company in 1438 (*see* page 139) but, in the sixteenth and seventeenth centuries, several corporations took advantage of the heralds' visitations to record their previously unauthorized arms, the first grant being that to the City of Gloucester in 1538.

The arms of many industrial towns and cities date from the Industrial Revolution. Sprigs of the cotton plant are found in the arms of Eccles and Darwen and in the crests of Bury and Burnley, as are shuttles, hanks and bales of cotton in other Lancashire towns. Similarly, fleeces and even goats appear in the arms of wool towns such as Leeds and Bradford.

The great railway companies of the Victorian Age adopted quasi-heraldic devices for use on locomotives and rolling stock, on station façades and tunnel keystones and in the fabrics and furnishings of their well-upholstered first-class carriages and waiting rooms – often at the expense of heraldic good taste. Most devices were combinations of the arms of towns served by the company (the Great Eastern adopted a radial design composed of the arms of Middlesex, Maldon, Ipswich, Norwich, Cambridge, Hertford, Northampton and Huntingdon, for example) while, north of the border, the Caledonian Railway appropriated the Royal Arms of Scotland! In 1897 the Manchester, Sheffield and Lincolnshire Railway changed its name to the Great Central and, in the following year, became the first railway company to be granted arms. Unfortunately, these 'official' arms were even more cluttered than the bogus ones adopted by many of their rivals.

The Industrial Revolution also created a new élite of manufacturing barons and iron masters anxious to acquire the trappings of gentility and with a voracious appetite for matters genealogical and heraldic. There was a substantial increase in the number of grants of arms made in the late eighteenth and nineteenth centuries, accompanied by a plethora of heraldic 'manuals' and a quite extraordinary level of genealogical activity, exemplified by the works of the ubiquitous Sir Bernard Burke.

1. Great Western Railway. Brass locomotive 'splasher' plate, mid 19C. 2. Coat of arms transfer, Great Central Railway. 3. Crest. Audenshaw UDC. 4. Arms of the City of Gloucester 1538. 5. Highland Railway coach transfer c. 1907. 6. Arms of the City of Leeds. 7. Crest, Atherton UDC. 8. Arms of the Borough of Darwen, Lancashire

Encouraged by the ostentatious excesses of civic pride and corporate rivalry, the use of unauthorized coats of arms flourished in the nineteenth century. The town of Crewe, for example, was but a single farmhouse before the arrival of the railway in 1841. To emphasize its newly-acquired civic status the council adopted bogus 'arms' which included pictures of a canal boat, a stage coach, a packhorse, a pillion and a railway locomotive!

Even properly authorized civic arms are generally more complex and contain a greater variety of charges than is usual in personal arms. Such devices are usually intended to represent historical as well as contemporary features of a civic authority and often allude to former industries. Locomotives are to be found in the arms of the railway towns of Darlington and Swindon, and in the arms of Morley in Yorkshire, a gold shuttle, a sprig of cotton and a miner's pick and shovel and two black *pellets* refer to wook, cotton and coal-mining. In the arms of Frome in Somerset, a teasel, used for raising the nap on cloth, recalls the town's ancient clothing industry, while an interlaced cross in the arms of Sherborne in Dorset commemorates both the abbey and the medieval weaving industry. Unfortunately, there is very often an understandable desire to include too much information in a civic coat of arms, thereby detracting from the aesthetic quality of the design. This was particularly true when a number of different authorities were combined: during the period of local government reorganization in 1974, for example.

Corporate arms also include those of schools, colleges and universities, public utilities, nationalized industries, public or limited liability companies, professional and sporting associations, guilds and fraternities, and learned and academic societies. The criteria for grants of arms to such bodies now appear to be stability and permanence as well as eminence. Many arms date from the Middle Ages: those of the original Livery Companies of the City of London, for instance, and the fifteenth-century arms of Oxford University (*Azure an open Book proper between three Crowns Gold*) which derive from the arms attributed by the medieval heralds to Edmund the Martyr, the ninth-century king of East Anglia (*see* page 14).

The use of supporters is reserved for corporate and civic bodies of particular eminence and distinction: the possession of an ancient charter, for example, which enabled the town council of Sherborne to obtain supporters in 1987, despite its parochial status.

Many institutions adopted the arms of their founders: as at Exeter College, Oxford (Walter de Stapledon, 1314) and St John's College, Oxford (Sir Thomas White, 1555).

Sherborne

1. Exeter College, Oxford
2. St John's College, Oxford
3. Oxford University
4. Borough of Swindon
5. Borough of Morley
6. Frome UDC

Ecclesiastical Heraldry

Ecclesiastical heraldry is distinctive for the manner in which colours and devices are often used to reflect religious concepts. As one might expect, the symbol of the cross is frequently found in ecclesiastical heraldry, though by no means exclusively so (*see* page 172). References to saints are common: the escallop shell in the arms of the bishopric of Rochester, for example, was the device of St Augustine, who founded the cathedral in 604, while the *saltire* on which it is placed is the familiar 'cross of St Andrew' to whom the church is dedicated. Many diocesan arms contain local allusions: those of Birmingham (granted in 1906) for instance, are divided *per pale indented* (vertically by an indented line) and refer to the nineteenth-century arms of the City of Birmingham which, in turn, were based on the arms of the medieval De Bermingham family. Similarly, the arms of the diocese of Truro include, on a black border, the fifteen *bezants* (gold roundels) of the Duchy of Cornwall.

Several diocesan arms contain references to the personal devices of former abbots or bishops. Those of the See of Hereford, for example, are derived from the arms of Thomas de Cantelope who was bishop from 1275 to 1282. The bishop's personal arms were *Azure three Leopard's Faces inverted jessant-de-lis Gold* (upside down and with *fleurs-de-lis* projecting from their mouths) but, in the diocesan arms, the field was changed to *Gules*.

Composite arms are of particular interest: those of Lincoln College, Oxford, for instance, refer to the college's history. They are *tierced in pale* (divided vertically into three) with the arms of the founder, Richard Fleming (1427), to the left and those of Thomas Scott (*alias* Rotherham), who re-endowed the College in the late fifteenth century, to the right. Both men were bishops of Lincoln and the diocesan arms are depicted between those of the two benefactors.

Both dioceses and cathedral chapters have their own arms and, although they may allude one to the other, they are not the same. The arms of the Dean and Chapter of Hereford Cathedral, for example, are *Gold five Chevronels Gules* – a reference to the Clare earls of Gloucester before 1313 who bore *Gold three Chevronels Gules*. Archbishops and bishops normally impale their personal arms with those of their sees. These combined coats are called arms of office.

In recent years, the College of Arms has devised arms for a number of American ecclesiastical foundations (*see* page 94). The arms of the Cathedral Church of the Advent at Birmingham, Alabama, for instance (1985) are gold and purple, the liturgical colour for Advent, and incorporate further symbols of Advent in the *Tau Cross* and motto 'Thy Kingdom Come'.

See of Rochester

See of Birmingham

City of Birmingham

Sir Foulke de Bermingham

See of Truro

See of Hereford

Lincoln College, Oxford

Dean and
Chapter of
Hereford
Cathedral

Cathedral Church
of the Advent
Birmingham
Alabama

The composition of an English Patent of Arms

1. Standard (optional when badges are granted)
2. Grantee's achievement of arms
3. Earl Marshal's arms
4. Sovereign's arms
5. Arms of the College of Arms
6. Margin decoration (optional)

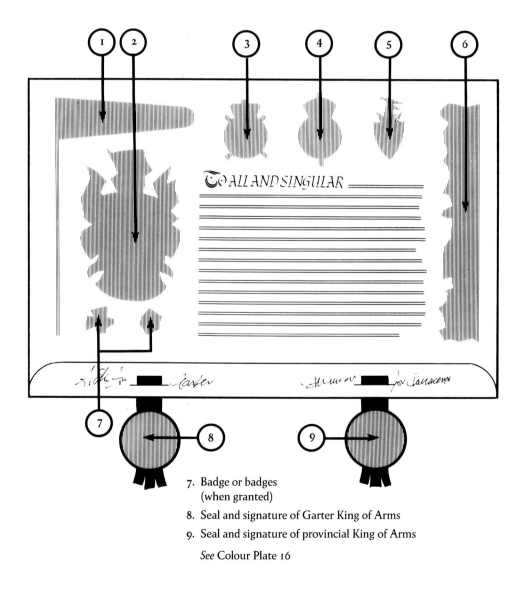

To all and singular

7. Badge or badges (when granted)
8. Seal and signature of Garter King of Arms
9. Seal and signature of provincial King of Arms

See Colour Plate 16

6   The Coat of Arms

A person may be armigerous – that is, entitled to bear arms – by confirmation or by grant. For arms to be confirmed, direct, legitimate, male-line descent from an armigerous ancestor must be established to the satisfaction of the Chapter of the College of Arms or, in Scotland, Lord Lyon. Once confirmed, pedigrees are recorded, thereby establishing the right of all members of the family to use the arms 'for ever hereafter ... with due and proper differences and according to the laws of Arms'.

A grant of arms is applied for either by means of a petition to the Earl Marshal or, in Scotland, to Lord Lyon who is empowered to grant arms to 'virtuous and well deserving persons'. Arms are a form of honour and, as such, emanate from the Sovereign. In England the authority to grant arms 'to eminent men' (which phrase includes also eminent women and corporations) is delegated to the kings of arms. In both countries a fee is required. Eligibility is not confined to those who have received some honour or decoration from the Crown, neither is it restricted to those who have held public office or a commissioned rank in the military services. Indeed, the term 'eminent' encompasses a broad spectrum of achievement.

Once eligibility has been established a warrant is issued by the Earl Marshal instructing the kings of arms to proceed. The design of the coat of arms is then agreed by the petitioner and the officer of arms acting on his behalf, and the letters patent prepared by the scriveners and herald painters. Of course, it is essential that the arms should be unique and the records are searched thoroughly before the design is finally approved by the kings of arms. Both the text of the patent and the arms as they appear in the letters patent are copied into the official records of the College of Arms to the satisfaction of the Registrar and the document is then signed and sealed by the kings of arms and finally delivered to the grantee. (*See* page 94 for Honorary Arms to eminent Americans.)

A coat of arms consists of a shield above which is a helmet, indicative of rank, to which a crest is attached by means of thongs or rivets, the unsightly join concealed by a wreath (or torse) of twisted silk. Sometimes a chapeau or crest coronet is used instead of (or in addition to) a wreath. From beneath the wreath hangs a mantling (or lambrequin) which was intended to protect the helmet from the elements. Peers may also depict their coronet of rank above the shield. Peers, senior knights of the orders of chivalry and some corporations are entitled to supporters. These are figures placed on either side of the shield and may be depicted standing on a compartment. There is usually a motto scroll either beneath the arms or (as in Scotland) above the crest.

There are, of course, different types of arms other than personal and marital arms. Arms of Adoption are those which have been assumed by someone who has no entitlement to them by descent: as the result of a Name and Arms clause in a will, for example, which requires the beneficiary to assume the name and arms of the testator as a condition of inheritance. Arms of Community, or impersonal arms, are those of a body corporate such as a civic authority or collegiate foundation. Arms of Concession are those conceded as a reward or used in conjunction with existing arms as an augmentation 'by mere grace': Richard II's grant of the attributed arms of Edward the Confessor to Thomas Mowbray, for example. Arms of Dominion (or Arms of Sovereignty) are those used by a sovereign within the territories over which he or she has dominion. Arms of Office are those borne in addition to personal arms by holders of certain offices: bishops, for instance, impale their personal arms with those of their see. Arms of Pretension are those borne to denote a claim to sovereignty, title, office or territory: the French quartering in the arms of Edward III, for example.

A blazon is a verbal or written description of armorial bearings using the conventions and terminology of heraldry (*see* page 142). Many terms are clearly derived from the (corrupted) French of thirteenth-century rolls of arms, but a large number of conventions were contrived by the heralds of 'the decadence' and, in the view of many armorists, are archaic and unnecessary. The objectives of blazon are brevity and precision. An accurate blazon is unambiguous and from it a coat of arms which is correct in every detail may be painted (emblazoned) or researched.

Letters patent are legal documents and blazons are therefore unpunctuated, except that the tinctures (colours) and charges begin with a capital letter. Adjectives (other than quantitative) follow the nouns they qualify, the tincture coming last: e.g. *a Lion salient Sable* [a leaping black lion].

AN ACHIEVEMENT OF ARMS – the principal elements

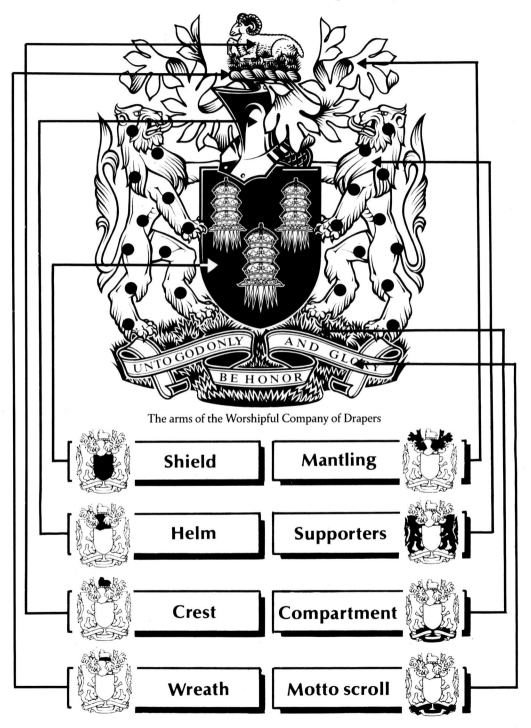

The arms of the Worshipful Company of Drapers

Shield

Mantling

Helm

Supporters

Crest

Compartment

Wreath

Motto scroll

The Shield

The shield is the essential element of a coat of arms and, with the banner, is the principal means of heraldic display.

In the eleventh century, and at the beginning of the twelfth, shields were long, narrow and kite-shaped, covering most of the body. They had rounded tops and were made of wood covered with tough, boiled leather. Such shields were in use at Hastings (1066) and during the First Crusade (1095–9), where raised edges, studs and bosses were often picked out in colour.

During the twelfth century the tops of shields became flatter, and decoration more personal. In the thirteenth century shields were shorter and were shaped like the base of a flat-iron (called a heater shield) and this style remained in use for heraldic purposes throughout most of the fourteenth century.

The increasing efficiency of the long bow, and the rapid development of plate armour, reduced the effectiveness of the shield as a means of defence and by the fifteenth century it had been abandoned by mounted knights except for heraldic purposes, notably at tournaments. It was at this time that the *à bouche* shield was most in evidence. This took a variety of forms but all had a small 'notch' cut in the side, apparently to allow for the free movement of a lance in the joust, though this may have been a stylistic affectation.

In the sixteenth century practical heraldry declined while heraldic display flourished. In order to accommodate numerous quarterings, shields of the period were almost invariably as broad as they were long. From the beginning of the seventeenth century many ornate shields found their way into heraldry, few of which could ever have been used on the battlefield. For the most part, these reflect contemporary architectural styles, the most common being the eighteenth-century 'tablet' shield and the popular nineteenth-century 'spade' shield. The beautifully proportioned 'heater' shield is that which is most often used in the present century, though the *à bouche* style is also popular.

The 'shield' in a woman's arms is conventionally depicted as a lozenge, there being an assumption that women did not make war or participate in tournaments and therefore had no practical use for a shield. For the same reason, women do not depict a helm and crest in their arms. The lozenge is such an unattractive and inconvenient shape that considerable artistic licence (and not a little ingenuity) is often required to accommodate the heraldry.

Shields

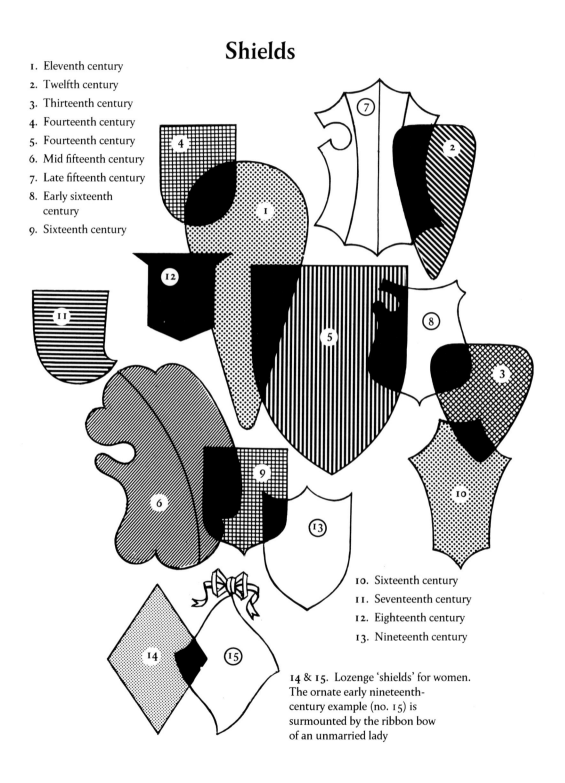

1. Eleventh century
2. Twelfth century
3. Thirteenth century
4. Fourteenth century
5. Fourteenth century
6. Mid fifteenth century
7. Late fifteenth century
8. Early sixteenth century
9. Sixteenth century

10. Sixteenth century
11. Seventeenth century
12. Eighteenth century
13. Nineteenth century

14 & 15. Lozenge 'shields' for women. The ornate early nineteenth-century example (no. 15) is surmounted by the ribbon bow of an unmarried lady

A charge is an object or geometrical figure depicted in relief on a shield of arms. Something is 'charged' when it has a charge placed upon it. In blazon, the lefthand side of a shield when viewed from the front is the *dexter* and the right is the *sinister*. Charges placed in the top portion of the shield are said to be *in chief* and those in the lower portion *in base*. There are three reference 'points' in a shield: *fess point* at the centre with *honour point* above and *nombril point* below.

The shield of arms may contain the impaled coats of a husband and wife (marital arms) or of an individual and those of his office (arms of office); a small central shield (an *inescutcheon* indicative of marriage to an heraldic heiress), or several different coats (quarterings) obtained through the accumulated marriages of ancestors to heraldic heiresses (*see* Chapter 8).

The senior dexter side is always described (blazoned) before the sinister in impaled arms, and in quartered arms each coat should be described separately and in the correct order, starting with that in *dexter chief* (the top left corner) and working across and down. The first coat is usually the principal (paternal) coat and may be repeated in the fourth quarter. When quarterings are themselves quartered they are described as *grandquarters*, the individual coats being *sub-quarters*. In such cases, each grandquarter is blazoned sub-quarter by sub-quarter before moving on to the next quartering.

A blazon should therefore open with a description of the layout of the shield e.g. *per pale* (for two coats), *quarterly* (for four) or *quarterly of six* [etc.] for more than four. Individual coats are then identified by number (e.g. *1st and 4th*) and blazoned.

The field (background) is first described: this may be a single tincture or comprise combinations of parted and varied fields (*see* pages 144–5).

The description of the field is followed by that of the principal charge, which is often an ordinary (*see* page 146) or heraldic beast, together with its attitudes and attributes (*see* page 170). Minor charges are then described, and any sub-ordinaries (*see* page 147), cadency marks or marks of distinction (*see* Chapter 8).

A shield may also be surrounded by a *bordure* or overlaid by a charge such as a *label, baton* or *canton*. These should be blazoned last, together with any charges placed upon them, the terms '*within*' or '*over all*' being used to describe their relationship to the other devices on the shield.

The order of blazon

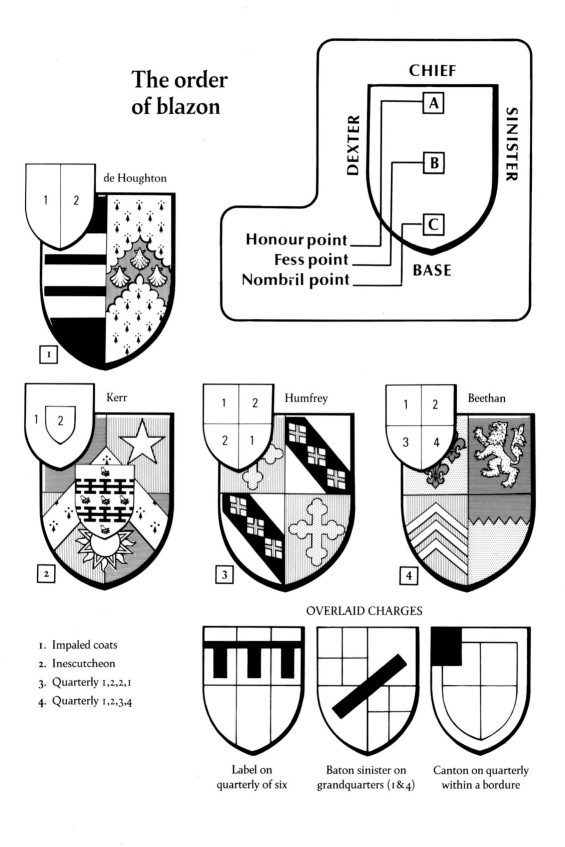

de Houghton

CHIEF

DEXTER

SINISTER

A

B

C

Honour point
Fess point
Nombril point

BASE

1

Kerr

2

Humfrey

3

Beethan

4

1. Impaled coats
2. Inescutcheon
3. Quarterly 1,2,2,1
4. Quarterly 1,2,3,4

OVERLAID CHARGES

Label on
quarterly of six

Baton sinister on
grandquarters (1 & 4)

Canton on quarterly
within a bordure

Parted Fields

The field (background) of a shield (or, indeed, of a charge) may be of a single tincture (colour) or comprise combinations of parted and varied fields.

A parted field is one that is divided by the principal lines of partition.

A varied field is composed of a series of geometrical divisions; usually six in number.

Unlike charges, neither parted nor varied fields are depicted in relief.

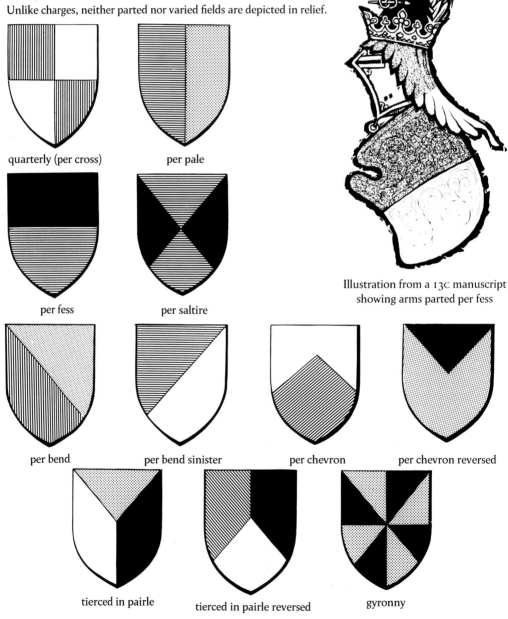

Illustration from a 13C manuscript showing arms parted per fess

quarterly (per cross)   per pale

per fess   per saltire

per bend   per bend sinister   per chevron   per chevron reversed

tierced in pairle   tierced in pairle reversed   gyronny

Varied Fields

Paly Argent and Gules
The arms of Ruthven, Earl of Gowrie

barry

bendy

bendy sinister

paly

chevronny

chequy

lozengy

barry bendy

paly bendy

gyronny of twelve

pily

pily bendy

pily bendy sinister

Ordinaries and their Diminutives

A principal charge of bold rectilinear shape is called an ordinary (or honourable ordinary) and a smaller charge, also of geometrical shape but subordinate to the ordinary or other principal charge, is a sub-ordinary.

Several of the ordinaries possess diminutives (such as *chevronels* and *bars*) while *cotises* are narrow diminutives placed parallel to the limbs of an ordinary.

It will be observed that the geometry of the ordinaries corresponds with that of the lines of partition (see page 144).

The inclination or disposition of charges (other than creatures) are described by reference to the geometry of the ordinaries e.g. *two Keys saltirewise* or *five Cinquefoils in saltire*.

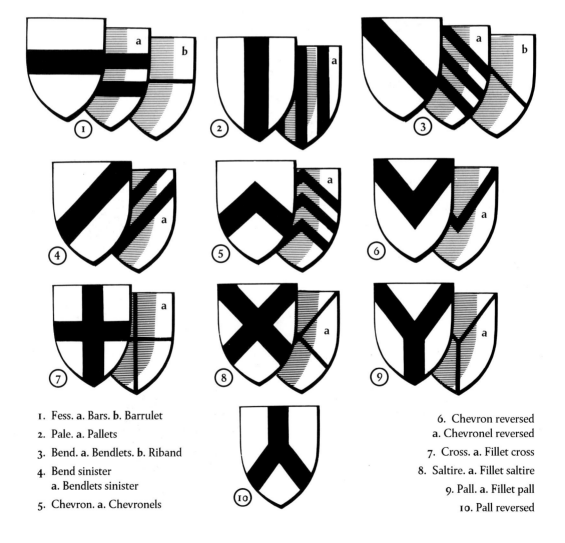

1. Fess. **a.** Bars. **b.** Barrulet
2. Pale. **a.** Pallets
3. Bend. **a.** Bendlets. **b.** Riband
4. Bend sinister
   a. Bendlets sinister
5. Chevron. **a.** Chevronels

6. Chevron reversed
   a. Chevronel reversed
7. Cross. **a.** Fillet cross
8. Saltire. **a.** Fillet saltire
9. Pall. **a.** Fillet pall
10. Pall reversed

Sub – Ordinaries

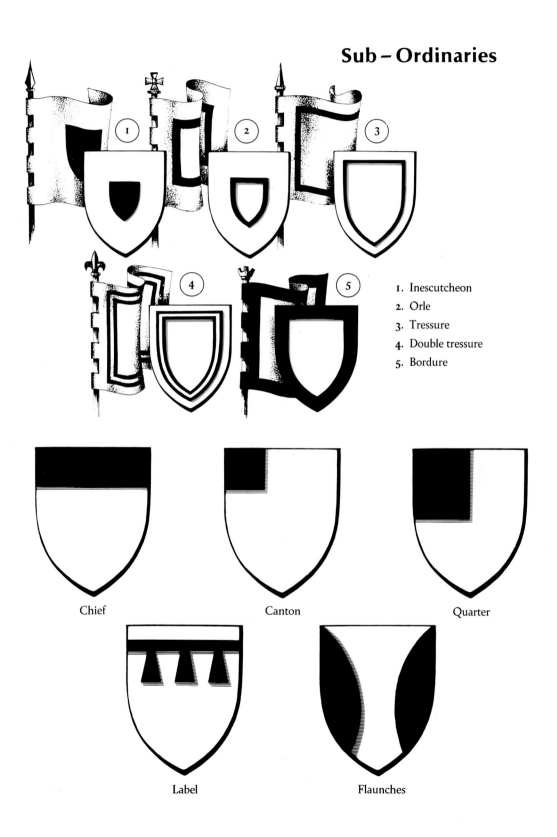

1. Inescutcheon
2. Orle
3. Tressure
4. Double tressure
5. Bordure

Chief

Canton

Quarter

Label

Flaunches

Varied Lines

Lines of partition, and those which delineate ordinaries and sub-ordinaries and the divisions of varied fields, may be straight or articulated in a variety of forms, each of which is possessed of its own term.

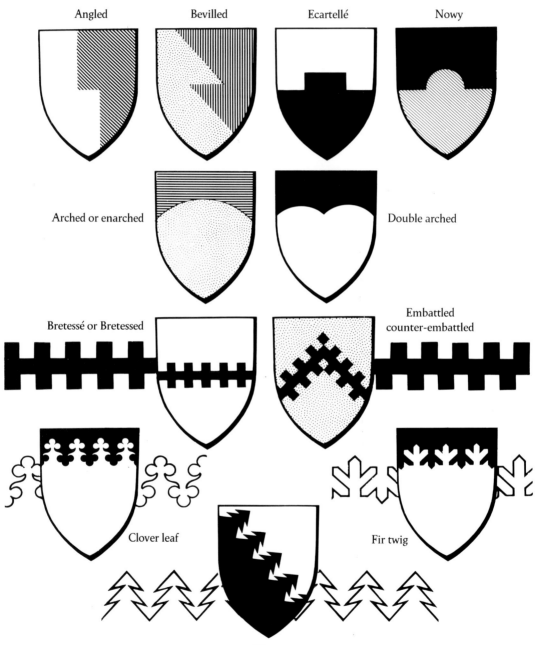

Angled

Bevilled

Ecartellé

Nowy

Arched or enarched

Double arched

Bretessé or Bretessed

Embattled
counter-embattled

Clover leaf

Fir twig

Fir tree

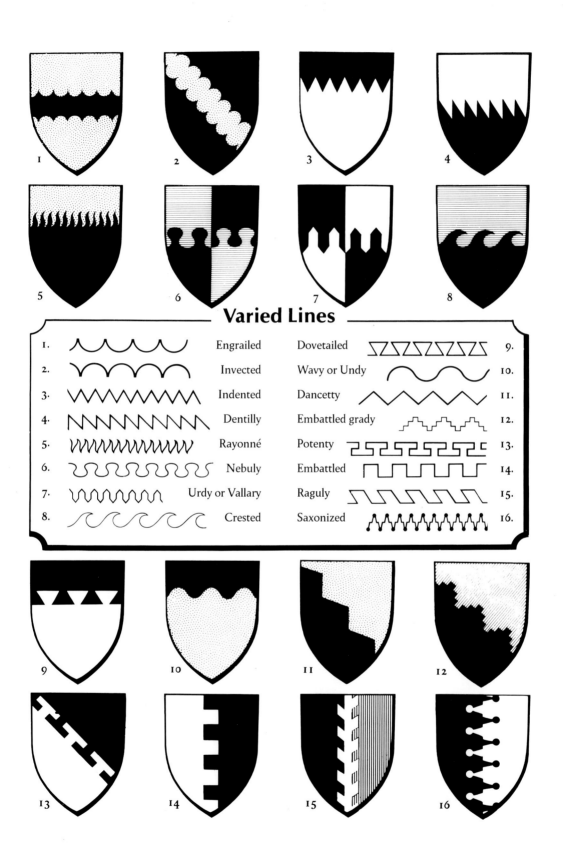

Varied Lines

1.	Engrailed	Dovetailed		9.
2.	Invected	Wavy or Undy		10.
3.	Indented	Dancetty		11.
4.	Dentilly	Embattled grady		12.
5.	Rayonné	Potenty		13.
6.	Nebuly	Embattled		14.
7.	Urdy or Vallary	Raguly		15.
8.	Crested	Saxonized		16.

The metals, colours and furs used in heraldry are known as tinctures.

The metals are *Or* (gold, often depicted as yellow) and *Argent* (silver, usually depicted as white).

The colours are *Gules* (red), *Azure* (blue), *Sable* (black), *Vert* (green), *Purpure* (purple) and *Murrey* (mulberry).

The so-called 'stains' are *Sanguine* (blood-red) and *Tenné* (tawny). These supposedly 'stain' the nobility of arms and are rare.

The most common furs, each of which is possessed of several variations, are *Ermine* (white with black 'tails') and *Vair* (white and blue 'pelts'). With the exception of *Potent*, the *Vair* variations are rare, as are *Plumeté* (feathers) and *Papelloné* (scales), though the latter is evident in a number of recent grants of arms.

Where a charge is represented in its natural colours it is described as *proper* e.g. *a Stag trippant* [walking] *proper*.

Metals and colours (but not furs) are subject to the tincture convention. This is the fundamental 'rule' of armory: that metal shall not lie on metal, nor colour on colour. This convention seems to have been universally accepted from the earliest times and is clearly intended to facilitate the accurate identification of heraldic devices at a distance. A blue cross on a silver field is clearer than a blue cross on black, for example. The convention applies only to charges that are placed *upon* a field or another charge. Adjacent divisions of varied or parted fields, for example, lie *next* to each other and do not break the 'rule'; neither do *bordures* (borders) or charges placed on varied or parted fields of alternating metal and colour. The rule does not apply to furs, though clearly a white charge on an *ermine* field would normally be avoided.

Exceptions will be found and these are usually brisures (marks of cadency – *see* Chapter 8) or augmentations of honour, intended to draw attention to an armiger whose service to his king was worthy of approbation (*see* page 42).

The tinctures of uncoloured coats of arms (those engraved on silver or in bookplates, for example) may often be determined by reference to the system of hatching developed by Sylvester Petra Sancta, a seventeenth-century writer on heraldry. In documents the tinctures may be shown by means of a 'trick' – a line drawing in which abbreviations are substituted for tinctures and numbers or letters for charges.

Metals, Colours & Furs

An heraldic 'trick'

Argent on a Chevron Gules
between three Lions rampant
Sable three Crescents Or

Petra Sancta hatchings

Or (gold)	Argent (silver)		
Gules (red)	Azure (blue)		
Vert (green)	Purpure (purple)		
Sable (black)	Murrey (mulberry)		
Tenné (tawny)	Sanguine (blood-red)		

Ermine	Ermines	Erminois	Pean

Vair	Counter-vair	Vair in pale
Vair en point	Potent	Counter-potent

Potent en point

Plumeté	Papelloné

The arms of the British Post Office
Gules billety bendy Argent four Bezants in fess

A number of small charges, evenly distributed over a field is described as semy, e.g.
Gules semy of Garbs Or (a red field 'powdered' with gold wheatsheaves).
Certain forms of semy have their own terms, though these may be found
with a variety of spellings (e.g. bezanté for bezanty)

Rutland　　　　　Empire Test Pilot's School　　　　　Lincoln's Inn

Vert semy of Acorns
a Horseshoe Or

Azure semy of Mullets Or
on a Pale Argent a Torch
enflamed Proper

Azure semy of Millrinds
and on a Canton Or a Lion
rampant Purpure

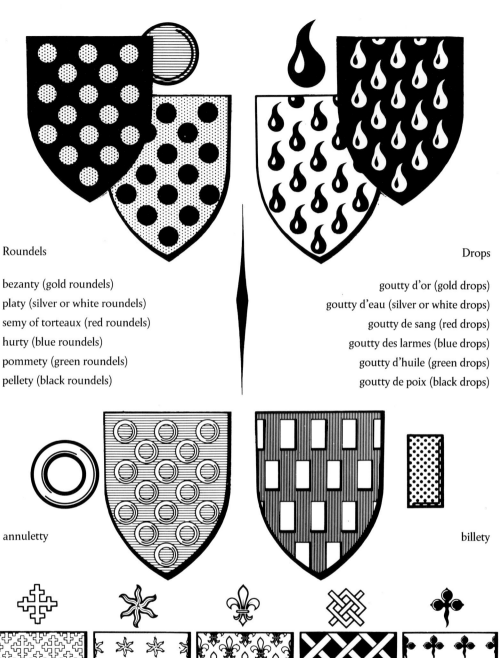

Roundels

bezanty (gold roundels)

platy (silver or white roundels)

semy of torteaux (red roundels)

hurty (blue roundels)

pommety (green roundels)

pellety (black roundels)

Drops

goutty d'or (gold drops)

goutty d'eau (silver or white drops)

goutty de sang (red drops)

goutty des larmes (blue drops)

goutty d'huile (green drops)

goutty de poix (black drops)

annuletty

billety

crusily

estoily

fleuretty
or semy-de-lis

fretty

treflé

The Helm and Crest

In the thirteenth and fourteenth centuries, when the helmet was an essential component of a knight's equipment, the cylindrical barrel or great helm, with a flat or rounded top, eye slits (sights) and ventilation holes (breaths), was invariably used in seals and other forms of heraldic display.

From the end of the fourteenth century this was superseded by the tilting helm which had no visor and was permanently 'closed', with only a slit for the eyes. It was, therefore, effective only when leaning forward in the tilting position. Tilting helms carried the ornate tournament crests of the period and were therefore associated with chivalric superiority – both in the lists and in coats of arms.

With the wholesale adoption of crests by the 'new gentility' of the Tudor period (see page 156) the nobility perceived a need for further differentiation in their arms and an extraordinary variety of bizzare and impracticable headgear began to appear in achievements of arms towards the end of the sixteenth century. By the early seventeenth century, these had been codified into a system in which different types of helm were assigned to armigers of different ranks – though, in Scotland, the great helm continued in general use. These were also stylized forms of tournament helms and, while they remain in use today, considerable artistic variations will be encountered, reflecting the heraldic tastes of intervening centuries.

The tilting helm was retained in the arms of gentlemen, esquires and corporations; the barriers helm, a fifteenth-century visored bascinet, was adopted for baronets and knights; and the mêlée helm, with its wide aperture for the face and protective bars or laticed grill, was reserved for peers. The late-fifteenth-century armet and sallet (or salade) may also be found, particularly in Scottish heraldry where the sallet is now used in civic heraldry.

Attached to the helm was the crest which, in the twelfth and thirteenth centuries, was a simple fan-like projection (the *crista* or cock's comb), the sides of which were painted with heraldic devices similar to those on the shield. These were succeeded by *panaches* of feathers which were often arranged in tiers. The ornate tournament crests of the high Middle Ages were moulded in light materials (paste board, cloth or boiled leather over a wooden or wire framework or basketwork) and were fastened to the helm by means of laces or rivets, the unsightly join concealed by a wreath or coronet or by the material of the crest itself, the lower edge of which formed a mantling, often in the form of a beast's fur or feathers.

1

2

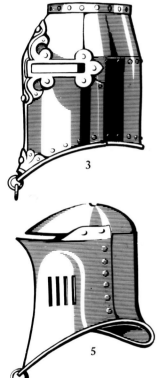

3

Armorial Helmets

1. Mêlée helm for peers, 15C
2. Barriers helm, 15C
3. & 4. Closed barrel helms, 14C
5. & 6. Tilting helms, 15C
7. Armet, late 15C
8. Sallet, late 15C
Top centre: Stylized helm
of the British sovereign

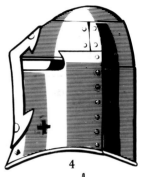

4

5

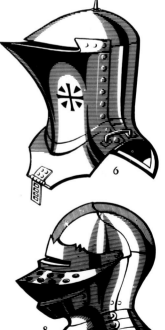

6

7

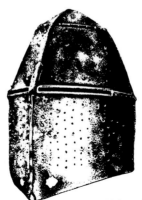

Great Helm of
Sir Richard Pembridge (d. 1375)
which once hung in
Hereford Cathedral

8

It is likely that, up to the late fifteenth century, crests were considered to be the perquisites of the knightly class: those who possessed the rank and resources that enabled them to participate in tournaments where crests were used. In the Middle Ages crests were hereditary and could be transmitted through heiresses, but it was not possible for them to be marshalled for display in the manner of quarterings (*see* Chapter 8) and consequently there are many instances of crests acquired through marriage being adopted in preference to paternal ones. For this reason many medieval crests are apparently unrelated to the devices depicted on the shield.

It was undoubtedly the case that the right to bear a crest was once considered to be a privilege and honour over and above the right to bear arms. It is hardly surprising, therefore, that encouraged by the heralds' visitations the Tudor gentry should have sought grants of crests with such rapacity. The practice of transmitting crests through heiresses ceased following the Restoration of 1660.

During the eighteenth and nineteenth centuries several crests were granted as augmentations – distinctive 'additions' to a coat of arms granted as a reward for distinguished service to the Crown.

The wreath (or torse) is a band of twisted strands of material worn about the medieval helmet as decoration and to conceal the base of the crest where it was laced or bolted to the tournament helm. The wreath probably originated in the ceremonial torse of the Dark Age rulers of western Europe and the colourful diadem of the Saracen. In heraldry, the wreath is conventionally depicted as having six visible twists of alternate tinctures, that to the left (the *dexter*) always being of a metal: *Or* [gold or yellow] or *Argent* [silver or white]. A crest and wreath are often depicted above a shield without helmet or mantling and, for peers, with a coronet of rank.

The mantling (or lambrequin) is a protective cloth affixed to the helmet and, in a coat of arms, is depicted as flowing from beneath the crest, sometimes terminating in tassels and scalloped or 'slashed' in stylized form. Almost certainly, the mantling originated in the Holy Land where it was worn by crusading knights to absorb the sun's heat, thereby preventing the helmet from becoming unbearably hot. It is surprising, therefore, that the inner lining of the mantling is always depicted as the lighter colour (*Argent* or *Or*).

1. A 14C 'fan' crest in the arms of the Schaler family (Basle)

2. Arms of Sir Nele Loryng with a panache of feathers. A 14C example based on the knight's Garter stall plate

3. 15C arms of Von Ramsperg von Rossno. A tournament helm with sculptured crest, wreath and mantling.
   From the Grünenberg *Wappenbuch*

Chapeaux & Crest Coronets

In the coats of arms of peers, coronets indicative of rank may be depicted immediately above the shield and beneath, or instead of, the helmet and crest. These coronets are the lineal descendants of the red velvet cap (*chapeau*) and gold circlet worn by the greater nobles in the Middle Ages (*see* page 114 and illustrations on pages 115 and 117).

Chapeaux are to be found in many coats of arms (notably those of the medieval period) where they are affixed to the helmet in place of a wreath. They are usually of red velvet and have an ermine lining which is turned up to form a brim ending in two 'tails' at the back. Today the *chapeau* is normally granted only to peers and, in Scotland, to feudal barons. Of course there are exceptions: the golden *chapeau* granted in 1990 to John Lancaster of Cheltenham, for example.

Ornamental circlets (crest coronets) are often found affixed to the helm in place of, or in addition to, a wreath and as such are an integral part of the crest. Confusingly, nearly all crest coronets are described as 'crowns' and, like the *chapeau*, they will also be encountered as charges.

In Scotland, civic coronets were granted to the old county and burghal councils and, from 1975, to the newly created regional, district, island and community councils.

Above: Arms and crested chapeau of Rose of Kilravock

Left: The crest of the Duke of Northumberland: a blue lion astride a chapeau of red velvet

Crest Coronets

Ancient Crown

Crown Vallary

Ancient Crown

Saxon Crown

Palisado Crown

Eastern Crown
(Scotland = Ancient Crown)

Mural Crown

Celestial Crown

Naval Crown

Astral Crown

Scottish Civic Coronets

Regional Council

District Council

Burghal

Community

County

Island Area

The arms of West Dorset
District Council with sea-wyvern
supporters and a compartment
of graded pebbles representing the
Chesil beach, a famous coastal
feature of West Dorset

Supporters & Compartments

Supporters are figures, usually beasts,
chimerical creatures or of human form,
placed on either side the shield to
'support' it. Unlike other elements in a
coat of arms, supporters have no practical origin
and cannot be traced with any certainty before
the fifteenth century. Though similar devices
may be found in early seals, where they occupy
the interstices between the shield and the outer
decorative border, their original pupose was
almost certainly decorative (*see* pages 21 and 85).
Others originated as personal devices which
were also used in seals and later translated into
badges and crests.

Supporters are granted to peers, knights of the
Garter, Thistle and (formerly) St Patrick and to
knights of the first class of other British orders of
chivalry. In Scotland, they are also granted to
chiefs of clans, certain knights and the heirs of
minor barons who sat in parliament prior to
1587 as of right. In Scotland, the heir apparent
may use his father's supporters, but not so in
England where, with the exception of hereditary
peers, they are not transmitted. In both
countries certain other families may claim an
ancient right to include supporters in their arms,
and they may be granted to eminent
corporations.

In a coat of arms, the base on which the
supporters are sometimes depicted is called a
compartment. This is usually a grassy mound
though it may take other, more appropriate,
forms such as the *graded pebbles* of the Chesil
beach in the arms of West Dorset District
Council or the *path of paving stones proper* in the
arms of the Police Federation of England and
Wales.

Supporters

1. Dexter supporter from the arms of Chesterfield Borough. 2. Lion passant guardant, dimidiating a ship's hull, an unusual supporter from the arms of Kent University. 3. Lizard supporter from the arms of the Ironmonger's Guild. 4. One of the crowned owl supporters from the arms of the City of Leeds. 5. Mermaid supporter, Borough of Boston arms. 6. Supporter from the arms of Cornwall County Council. 7. Antelope from the arms of the Standard Bank

Mottoes

Mottoes, accompanying signatures, may be found in medieval documents and manuscripts and first appear in heraldry in the fourteenth century, though they were not in general use until the seventeenth century.

It seems likely that many early mottoes were used, perhaps in abbreviated form, as *cris-de-guerre*, to rally troops in the field of battle: ESPÉRANCE (Percy), for example. This appears to have been the practice in Scotland where the slogan (or slughorn) is the battle cry of the chief of a clan or house, as in I DAR (Dalzell) and GANG WARILY (Drummond). It is not without significance that mottoes often appeared on standards, the great medieval livery flags beneath which military levies were mustered (*see* page 60). Clearly, it was considered important that troops should be familiar with their leader's war-cry before taking the field.

A motto is an aphorism, the interpretation of which is often obscure but may allude to a name, a charge in the arms, to the crest or to some event in a family's history: TOUCH NOT THE CAT BOT A GLOVE (referring to the cat crest of The Mackintosh) and I SAVED THE KING (Turnbull), for example.

In Scotland, the slogan is depicted on a scroll above the crest, on the circlet of a crest badge and, if there is more than one motto, on an additional scroll beneath the shield. In England mottoes are usually depicted on a scroll beneath the shield. Whereas in England they may be changed at will, and are not specified in the letters patent by which arms are granted or confirmed, in Scotland they are both specified and re-matriculated by succeeding generations of armigers.

Mottoes may be in any language. In the past Latin and French were favoured but there is a growing preference for native languages: the Cornish OLL AN ELETH WYN GANSO ('All the Holy Angels with Him') of the Reverend Mark Elvins of Brighton, for example, and UMLIMU LELIZWE ('God and Country') a motto in the Sinderbele language of the Matabele tribe of Zimbabwe, in the arms of Cooper of Pietermaritzburg.

Mottoes lend themselves to anagrams or may conceal a surname as in SINCERITAS COMES SERMONIS SIT ('May sincerity be the companion of conversation'), the motto of Michael Messer of Bath; AS MAN SOWS SO SHALL HE REAP, the motto of David Asman of Fairlawn, New Jersey; and CAVE CANEM ('Beware of the dog') the motto of Raymond Cave of Ludlow, which also refers to the Cave crest of a *Greyhound courant Sable collared Argent*.

Motto Scrolls and Scots clan badges

1. Scottish arms of Johnstone, Marquess of Annandale showing typical motto scroll above the crest

2. Clan badge of Drummond with the clan slogan encircling the crest on a strap and buckle

3. Motto scroll entwining the ostrich feather device of Henry Bolingbroke (the future Henry IV c. 1366–1413)

Above: The famous Bedford flag, an American banner borne at the battle of Concord during the revolution of 1775. Originally painted in England in the 17C, it was the cavalry standard of Three County Troop, eastern Massachusetts

Common charges

LIONS AND EAGLES

Right: Arms of Sir Simon de Felbrigge from his Garter stall-plate in St George's Chapel, Windsor, *c.* 1442. The lion is turned to the sinister to face the high altar

Below: Lion passant guardant

Eagle shield from the chantry of Abbot Ramrydge (d. 1542) at St Albans

Double-headed eagle ducally gorged, with wings displayed. A supporter in the arms of the city of Salisbury

7 Common Charges

In the Middle Ages, the lion was considered to be the embodiment of courage, strength and nobleness, the King of Beasts and a fitting symbol of kings and princes. One of the earliest examples of hereditary arms is that of William Longespée, natural son of King Henry II, who bore six gold lions on a blue shield as did his grandfather, Geoffrey of Anjou (*see* page 27). In early heraldry, what is now a *lion passant guardant* was described as a leopard (hence 'the leopards of England' in the royal arms), indeed any lion that was not *rampant* was blazoned *leopardé*. According to the bestiaries, lion cubs were born dead and remained so for three days whereupon their father breathed into their faces and gave them life. For this reason, the lion is associated with Christ risen from the dead and is often depicted in church carvings as fighting with the devil in a dragon's form. The lion is of such a noble and compassionate nature that he will not attack a stricken man and is angered only when wounded. He fears nothing except a white cockerel and if he is sick he is cured by eating a monkey.

The eagle was the standard of the Roman legion. In armory it is considered to be pre-eminent among the birds, and Charlemagne is said to have adopted an eagle as his device when he was crowned Holy Roman Emperor in AD 800. Until recently, lecterns in the form of eagles were to be found in nearly every church; with wings open as in flight they carried forth the Word and the Light of the Gospel. The eagle's suitability for such a task is explained in the medieval *Book of Beasts*: 'When the eagle grows old and his wings become heavy and his eyes become darkened with a mist, then he goes in search of a fountain, and, over against it, he flies up to the height of heaven, even into the circle of the sun [symbolizing Christ], and there he singes his wings and at the same time evaporates the fog of his eyes in a ray of the sun. Then at length taking a header down into the fountain, he dips himself three times in it, and instantly he is renewed with a great vigour of plumage and splendour of vision.' (trans. T. H. White, London, 1954)

Chimerical Creatures

Most chimerical creatures arrived in European heraldry through the medieval bestiaries and many originated in classical mythology. The *centaur*, for example, which has the body and legs of a horse and a man's trunk, arms and head (when holding a bow and arrow it is termed *sagittary* or *sagittarius*); the *pegasus*, the beautiful flying horse of the Knights Templar, which became the symbol of fame, eloquence and contemplation; and the *salamander* which, when frightened, would exude a milky substance that moistened its skin and enabled it to extinguish fire.

The *tyger* has the body of a wolf with a thick mane, a lion's tail, massive, powerful jaws and a pointed snout. The tyger comes from Hyrcania and was famed for its swiftness by the Persians who named their river after it. The female tyger was a devoted mother but could be deprived of her young by placing looking glasses in her way 'whereat she useth to long to gaze … and so they escape the swiftness of her pursuit'. Because of this the tyger is often depicted gazing into a mirror. The *alphyn* is similar to the tyger but stockier and with tufts of hair on its body and a thick mane. It has a long thin tongue, long ears and a knotted tail. The heraldic *antelope* has a tyger's head, tusks, serrated horns, an antelope's body, a tufted spine and a lion's tail.

The Egyptian *phoenix* was believed to live for five centuries. At the approach of death it would fly to Arabia and hide itself in a nest of sweet-smelling spices which burst into flames when fanned by the bird's wings. The phoenix was burned to ashes but after three days a small worm appeared which grew into a new phoenix. Inevitably, it was adopted as a Christian symbol of resurrection and immortality.

The *griffin* combines the attributes of the king of beasts and the king of birds. It has the body and ears of the lion and the head, wings and talons of the eagle. It was associated with the gods of Minos and Greece and was an animal of the sun and of justice and was the guardian of treasure. There is in heraldry a separate beast called the *male griffin* which dates from the post-medieval period. This has no wings but spikes protrude from its body like rays.

The heraldic *panther* is termed *incensed*: having flames issuing from its ears and mouth. In the bestiaries it is described as being both beautiful and kind, and when it awakes from sleep 'a lofty sweet singing comes from his mouth and … a delightful stream of sweet-smelling breath' that all other animals follow – excepting the dragon, who runs away and hides in fear.

CREATURES

1. Sagittary or sagittarius. 2. Tyger.
3. Pegasus. 4. Griffin. 5. Alphyn.
6. Antelope. 7. Panther. 8. Phoenix.
9. Salamander.

continued on page 169

Traditionally, the *pelican* is devoted to her young and is frequently depicted piercing her breast (*vulning herself*) in order that they should be revived by her blood. Thus the pelican became a mystic emblem of Christ, whose blood was shed for mankind. When depicted *vulning herself*, and nourishing her young while standing on the nest, the pelican is described as being *in her piety*.

The medieval *unicorn* of western Europe is an elegant and beautiful animal, like a horse but with cloven feet, a lion's tail, a goat's beard and a delicate spiralling horn on its forehead. It became a symbol of Christ because of its purity and virtue and to its horn were ascribed medicinal powers of healing and purification.

In a twelfth-century bestiary the *yale* is described as being the size of a horse and having the tusks of a boar and extremely long horns that could be moved as required – either singly or together – to meet aggression from any direction.

In appearance, the *martlet* is similar to the house martin, swallow and swift, but is depicted without feet or claws for the bestiaries claimed that it lived its entire life in the air and had no need to touch the ground.

Originally, all scaly creatures with bat-like wings were 'dragons': depicted as serpents, without legs or sometimes with just two. With the arrival in the late medieval bestiaries of a four-footed version, a distinction came to be made between the *wyvern* (with two legs) and the *dragon* (with four). The dragon probably entered British heraldry as the standard of the Roman cohort and remained in the symbolism of the post-Roman era, notably in the 'burning dragon' of Cadwallader. Although the wyvern of mythology typifies viciousness and envy, and became the symbol of pestilence and plague, in heraldry it is used as a symbol for overthrowing the tyranny of a demonic enemy.

The *cockatrice* is hatched on a dunghill from a cock's egg by a serpent. It is so venomous that its look or breath are lethal to all other creatures – except for the weasel. At the age of nine years, the cockatrice will lay an egg on a midden and a toad will come to hatch it and produce, not another cockatrice, but a *basilisk* which has a dragon's head at the end of its tail. So dreadful is its appearance that should it catch sight of its reflection it will instantly burst with horror.

During the post-medieval period many strange creatures were added to the heraldic zoo, often by the interbreeding of their medieval forebears to produce a singularly unattractive (and rare) collection of armorial hybrids.

CREATURES cont'd

10. Pelican in her piety.
11. Unicorn. 12. Wyvern.
13. Cockatrice. 14. Dragon. 15. Martlets.
16. Yale.

Beasts and chimerical creature are depicted in a variety of attitudes, the most common of which are here illustrated. Others include:

addorsed back to back
affronty facing the observer
caboshed a head *affronty* but without a neck
close wings folded
combatant rampant and facing one another
conjoined joined together
contourné facing the *sinister*
courant running
coward tail between legs
diplayed wings expanded
embowed curved
endorsed back to back

enfiled passing through
ensigned having a charge placed above
forcene a rearing horse
guardant looking at the observer
haurient of a fish, head upwards
naiant swimming
nowed knotted
reguardant looking over the shoulder
segreant a griffin when *rampant*
trippant a walking stag
urinant diving
volant flying horizontally
vorant devouring

In blazon, the attributes of heraldic charges are often self-evident (e.g. *beaked, bristled, chained, collared* etc). Others include:

annelled ringed (e.g. a bull)
armed of talons, claws etc.
attired of antlers
barbed of an arrow head or sepals of a rose
couped severed in a straight line
crined of hair or a mane
doubled with the lining turned up
embattled having crenellations
embrued spattered or dripping with blood
en soleil surrounded by rays of the sun
eradicated uprooted
erased torn off roughly
fourché forked

fructed bearing fruit
gorged encircled about the throat
habited clothed
incensed flames issuing from mouth and ears
jessant issuing from
langued of the tongue
masoned of the mortar of masonry
membered of the legs of a bird
pierced with a circular hole
queued tailed
unguled of hoofs
vested clothed
voided depicted in outline
vulned wounded

Passant

Couchant

Salient

Rampant

Sejant

Statant

Dormant

The CROSS

There are innumerable charges used in heraldry, ranging from the ubiquitous *fleur-de-lis* to the unique urinal crest of Dr Louys Caerlyon (1483). But by far the most common charge is the cross, the universal symbol of the Christian Church, though a device which pre-dates Christianity by many centuries.

The preponderance of crosses in armory reflects both the influence of the Crusades and medieval man's preoccupation with his religion. According to various sources there are between three and five hundred different types of cross to be found in armory, though of these only about twenty or so are in regular use and are here illustrated. There can be little doubt that the earliest heraldic crosses were of the simplest kind and that the proliferation of variants resulted from casual embellishment and the desire of the post-medieval heralds to define forms which had been arrived at by artistic licence. Even today, new forms may be introduced though the heraldic authorities seem reluctant to acknowledge them by name. For example, the *Saxon Cross* devised by the author for the arms of West Dorset District Council is described in the letters patent as *A Mullet of four points each point terminating in a Roundel* (see page 160).

Crosses that are *fitched* (also *fitchy* or *fitché*) have a pointed lower limb, whereas a cross *fitched at the foot* has a lower limb terminating in a point.

1. Recercely
2. Bottony
3. Cross-crosslet
4. Tau (St Anthony's)
5. Fourché
6. Celtic
7. Potent
8. Potent quadrate
9. Fylfot or cramponned
10. Formy fitchy
    at the foot

11. Cross-crosslet
    fitchy
12. Moline
13. Saxon
14. Patriachal
15. Flory
16. Patonce
17. Formy or paty
18. Fleuretty
19. Formy fitchy
20. Maltese

Heraldic Flora

The natural world of trees, plants and flowers is well represented in heraldry. In the Middle Ages such devices were usually stylized but several recent grants have included the native flora of an armiger's country.

When the roots of a tree are depicted it is said to be *eradicated*, when fruit is shown it is *fructed* and when a branch is broken it is *fracted*. A gold *stock* or tree-stump device was adopted by Edward III in allusion to his manor of Woodstock in Oxfordshire (*see* colour plate 3).

The heraldic rose has five petals and is of the sweet briar or dogrose variety. Roses may be described as *barbed and seeded proper* when the green sepals appear between the petals and the seeds are gold. When a rose (or other flower) is depicted with a stem and leaves it is blazoned *slipped and leaved*. The famous Tudor rose combined, in a variety of forms, the red and white roses of York and Lancaster (*see* page 78) and the white *rose en soleil* was a badge of the House of York (*see* page 54).

A *cinquefoil* is a stylized plant with five petals or leaves. If it has a hole at the centre it is said to be *pierced* and it may have a stalk, in which case it is *slipped*. There are several variants including the *trefoil* (with three petals or leaves), the *quatrefoil* (four) and the *sixfoil* and *octofoil* (eight).

The *fleur-de-lis* (also *fleur-de-lys*) is a stylized form of the Madonna Lily (*Lilium candidum*). A field of *fleur-de-lis* is blazoned *semy-de-lis* and there are crosses *fleuretty* and *flory*, both of which have limbs terminating in fleurs-de-lis (*see* page 173). The term *flory* may be used to describe any charge that is decorated with *fleurs-de-lis*: the *double tressure* in the royal arms of Scotland, for example, which is *flory counter-flory* (*see* page 106).

Other common charges are the *garb* which is a sheaf of wheat (unless another type of grain is specified) and the *chaplet* or *garland* which is a circular wreath of leaves and flowers, usually heraldic roses.

Rose slipped and leaved

Fleur-de-lis

Trefoil

Quatrafoil

Cinquefoil

Opposite page. Left: Tudor acorn and oak leaf device. *Right:* The badge of Sir Wyllm. Kyngyston 1539
This page. Top left: Elizabethan pomegranate. *Top centre:* Device from the seal of Robert Fitz-Pernell, Earl of Leicester d. 1206.
Top right: Columbine badge of Care.
Centre: Gold stock device adopted by Edward III

Garb

Rose within
a chaplet of
oak leaves

Miscellaneous Charges

The definition of ordinaries and sub-ordinaries (*see* pages 146–7) has always been a matter of debate, indeed many armorists question the need for such distinctions. The *pile*, for example, appears in several lists of ordinaries and the *label* (the cadency mark of an eldest son) is often defined as a sub-ordinary. Both are illustrated here among a variety of other geometrical charges including the *billet*, *fret*, *gemel* (now blazoned as a *bar gemel*), *mullet*, *shakefork* and *lozenge*, together with its heraldic cousins the *fusil*, *mascle* and *rustre*.

Roundels (flat, coloured discs) are common charges and are often blazoned simply as (e.g.) *a Roundel Gules*. However, each has its own term: *bezant* (from the gold coin of Byzantium), *plate* (silver), *hurt* (a blue 'bruise'), *torteau* (red), *pellet* or *ogress* (black), *pomme* or *pomeis* (green), *golpe* (a purple 'wound') and the *fountain* which is *barry wavy Argent and Azure* (*see also* page 153).

There are numerous charges which represent everyday items in stylized form. The *maunch*, for instance, is a medieval sleeve, cut off at the shoulder and with a long lappet tapering from the cuff. A *water-bouget* is a stylized yoke supporting two leather waterbags, the best-known example being in the allusive arms of Bourchier: *Argent a Cross engrailed Gules between four Water-bougets Sable* (*see* colour plate 2). Another common charge, the *millrind* or *fer-de-moline*, is the iron centrepiece of a millstone while the *clarion* was probably a portable wind-instrument. Like many other stylized charges, the *maunch*, *bouget*, *millrind* and *clarion* will be found depicted in a variety of forms, as will the surgeon's *fleam* (lancet) and the farrier's *barnacle* (or *brey*) which was used to curb a horse.

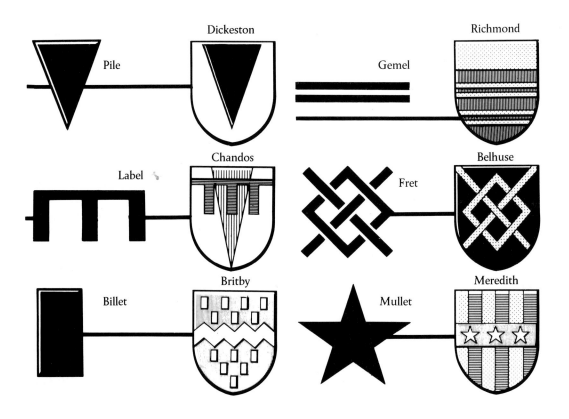

Pile — Dickeston — Gemel — Richmond

Label — Chandos — Fret — Belhuse

Billet — Britby — Mullet — Meredith

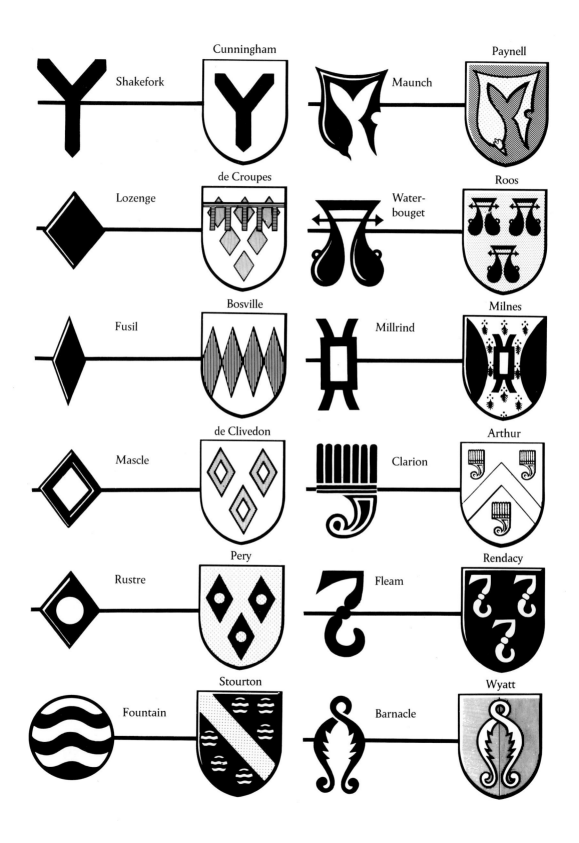

Shakefork   Cunningham

Maunch   Paynell

Lozenge   de Croupes

Water-bouget   Roos

Fusil   Bosville

Millrind   Milnes

Mascle   de Clivedon

Clarion   Arthur

Rustre   Pery

Fleam   Rendacy

Fountain   Stourton

Barnacle   Wyatt

Considerable artistic licence may be exercised when depicting heraldic devices. As a consequence, no two interpretations of a blazon are the same and the art of heraldry is extraordinarily rich and varied.

Many charges originated in objects that would have been familiar to our medieval ancestors and are depicted in stylized form. A *beacon* is a fire-bucket on a pole, reached by means of a ladder, while the *square beacon* crest of the Phelips family of Montacute is a simple metal fire basket. The *caltrap* is a pointed, iron 'cheval trap' several of which were strewn on the ground to impede a cavalry charge. A *pheon* is a barbed arrowhead, conventionally depicted with the point downwards, and the *escarbuncle* (or *carbuncle*) originated in the ornamental bosses of early shields. The *fleece* is a horned ram depicted as though suspended from a hook by means of a band and ring and the *woolpack* has the appearance of a bulky cushion with the corners tied. The *sun* is conventionally depicted with alternating straight and wavy rays, symbolizing light and heat, while a *sunburst* consists of rays issuing from behind a cloud. The sun is often blazoned as a *sun in splendour* and may have a human face. Stars are six-pointed *estoiles* and the *moon*, which may also have a face, is said to be *in plenitude* or *in her complement* when full. The *crescent* is a common charge and may be *increscent* or *decrescent*.

Beacon

Square beacon

MORE COMMON CHARGES

1. Escarbuncle. 2. Sunburst. 3. Fleece.
4. Woolpack. 5. Crescent (b. Decrescent.
c. Increscent). 6. Caltrap. 7. Sun in splendour.
8. Pheon. 9. Estoile.

COMPOUND ARMS

John de Dreux

DIMIDIATED ARMS

Youghal Ireland

Seal of Margaret
Queen of Edward I

IMPALED ARMS

Bardolf/Poynings

ESCUTCHEON OF PRETENCE

Fitzwilliams

8 Marshalling and Cadency

The practice of arranging heraldic devices to signify marriage, inheritance or the holding of an office is known as marshalling.

Early forms of marshalling are evident in a number of thirteenth-century seals where a figure is depicted between shields bearing arms of alliance or where a geometrical arrangement of related shields surrounds that of the principal house.

Another early method was by compounding charges from several different shields to form an entirely new one: the arms of John de Dreux, Duke of Britanny and Earl of Richmond, for example, whose mother was a daughter of Henry III, bore a shield charged with the gold and blue chequers of de Dreux within a red border charged with the gold lions of England and *over all a Canton Ermine* for Brittany.

From *c.*1300 different coats were marshalled in the same shield, at first by means of dimidiation: the dexter half of a husband's arms being joined to the sinister half of his wife's. But this practice often resulted in alarming visual ambiguities and it was abandoned in favour of impalement, by which two complete coats were placed side by side in the same shield.

Impalement generally signifies a temporary or non-hereditary combination of arms, such as arms of office and those of a husband and a wife who is not an heraldic heiress but whose father is armigerous. But a woman who has no brothers living and no nephews or nieces from deceased brothers becomes her father's heraldic heiress upon his death. While he lives her arms are impaled with her husband's, but when her father dies they are displayed on an escutcheon of pretence in the centre of her husband's shield. If she has sisters, each is a co-heiress, and each transmits her father's arms on equal terms.

After a woman's death, her husband ceases to bear his wife's escutcheon of pretence, and her children quarter their arms by dividing the shield into four and placing the paternal arms in the first and fourth quarters and the maternal arms in the second and third. Thereafter, further inherited arms may be added as 'quarterings', usually in order of acquisition.

Quartered coats may themselves be quartered and in such cases the principal quarterings are called grand quarters and the subsidiary ones sub-quarters. This method of marshalling, which is called counter-quartering or sub-quartering, continues in Scotland but not in England.

Many armigers accumulated a large number of coats, sometimes adding ones which were already present in their arms through earlier marriages with heiresses of the same family. It is not necessary to retain all the coats that have been acquired in this way, indeed it is often impracticable to display more than four. But when a selection is made it is necessary to in-clude those coats by which the selected ones were acquired. For example, were an armiger able to prove Mowbray descent through a fairly humble ancestor called Smith, and thereby entitlement to the Mowbray arms, it would be necessary to include the Smith coat in order to justify the use of the more illustrious arms of Mowbray.

A widow continues to use her late husband's arms, but on a lozenge and without helm or crest, and with her own arms either impaled or in pretence. If she is the widow of a peer she may continue to use supporters and the appropriate coronet of rank. In Scotland, a widow whose paternal family is not armigerous may display her late husband's arms with a silver knotted *cordelière*. If a widow remarries, she no longer uses the arms of her first husband.

A widower ceases to use his late wife's arms except on memorials and hatchments (*see* page 98). If he remarries he may use the arms of *both* wives, for commemorative purposes, in the sinister half of his shield: either one above the other (with the arms of his first wife *in chief*) or side by side (with his first wife's arms to the *dexter*).

Unmarried women are entitled to bear their father's arms in a lozenge, but not his crest. A divorced woman reverts to her maiden arms which, again, are borne in a lozenge, and these may be charged with a *mascle* (a voided diamond) to indicate that she is a divorcée.

QUARTERING

The arms of Heneage Mackenzie Griffin Esq.

Quarterly of 8: 1. Griffin. 2. Favell. 3. de la Warre.
4. Latimer. 5. Braybroke. 6. Ledette.
7. Foliott. 8. Rayncourt.

Grand and Sub-quarters

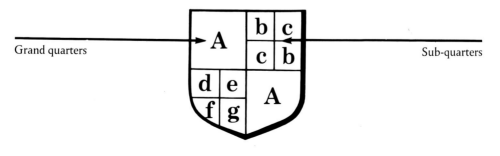

Grand quarters   Sub-quarters

Cadency

The first principle of heraldry is 'one man one coat' and the requirement that all cadet members of a family should bear distinctive arms is known as cadency.

Since the fifteenth century, small charges (*brisures*) have been used to denote cadency in English heraldry. The three-pointed *label* of the eldest son, depicted in the upper half of the shield, is discarded on the death of the head of the family, the heir using the undifferenced arms; while the brisures of younger sons are usually placed centrally or at the top of the shield and may deliberately contravene the tincture convention in order to distinguish them from other charges (*see* page 150).

In succeeding generations the brisure itself should (theoretically) be charged with a further mark of difference: for example, the fourth son of a third son would have a *martlet* on a *mullet*; the second son of a second son would bear a *crescent* on a *crescent*, and so on. Such a system is clearly absurd and it is hardly surprising that it has rarely survived a second generation. Brisures are hereditary to all legitimate descendants in the male line, though they may be dispensed with when quarterings are added, thereby making the arms distinctive from those of the senior branch.

In the Middle Ages, a *label* of three or five points was usually the mark of an eldest son as it is today. But no system of brisures was then in common use and cadency was often indicated by amending the paternal arms or by the addition of minor charges.

In Scottish heraldry there is no such thing as 'family arms': undifferenced arms are borne only by Heads of Clans or Chiefs of a Family or Name. In Scotland, it is an offence to bear arms unless they have been matriculated with Lord Lyon King of Arms and entered into the Public Register of All Arms and Bearings in Scotland. Matriculation is not simply registration; the process requires the correct marshalling of the arms, together with the appropriate brisures indicating relationships within an armigerous family. Armorial bearings are succeeded to by the heir while cadets, the younger sons of the armiger and progenitors of subsidiary branches of a family, are assigned amended versions of their paternal arms when they re-matriculate with Lord Lyon. These descend to their children on matriculation, again with appropriate differences. A system of *bordures* is used for this purpose by succeeding generations and this allows the degree of kinship to the main branch of the family to be shown.

ENGLISH CADENCY MARKS

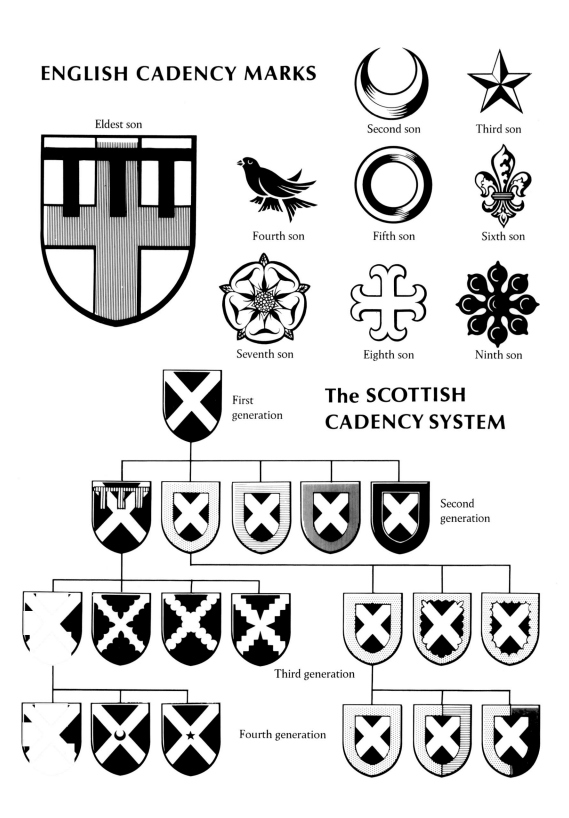

Eldest son

Second son

Third son

Fourth son

Fifth son

Sixth son

Seventh son

Eighth son

Ninth son

The SCOTTISH CADENCY SYSTEM

First generation

Second generation

Third generation

Fourth generation

Marks of Distinction

The medieval concept of bastardy and the use of special heraldic devices to signify illegitimacy continue to attract debate.

Although in English heraldry such marks are sometimes described as 'abatements of honour' which 'debruise' a coat of arms, in the Middle Ages they often signified a blood relationship with a member of the nobility and were therefore considered to be 'marks of distinction'. Neither did they necessarily imply the illegitimacy of the armiger who bore them; often they were intended to indicate, not that he was personally illegitimate, but that he was not in legitimate line of succession.

Many methods were used to denote illegitimacy in medieval heraldry: altering the composition of the paternal shield, for example, or devising new arms using a father's badges or the devices in his shield.

The much-loved but erroneous 'bar sinister' of the popular press was, in fact, the *bendlet sinister* which was widely used for this purpose down to the eighteenth century when it was superseded by the *bordure wavy*. In Scotland it is the *bordure compony* that is reserved to indicate illegitimacy.

The *baton sinister* (a different charge, though with a confusingly similar name to the *bendlet sinister*) has almost invariably been used to denote illegitimacy in the English royal family, though again there have been notable exceptions particularly during the Middle Ages. Sir Roger Clarendon, bastard son of the Black Prince, for instance, bore his father's *ostrich feather* badges on a black *bend* (*see* page 40) and for Sir John de Clarence, son of Thomas, Duke of Clarence, the royal devices and colours of his father's arms were rearranged in a shield *Per chevron Gules and Azure in chief two Lions combatant and in base a Fleur-de-lis Gold*. The Beauforts, the illegitimate line of John of Gaunt and Katherine Swynford, at first adopted a shield parted *per pale Argent and Azure* (the Lancastrian colours) *on a Bend Gules three Lions of England and a Label of France* but, following their legitimation in 1397, they used the royal arms within a blue and white *bordure*.

Marks of distinction may be granted by means of a royal licence. If, for example, an illegitimate child can prove paternity, or if paternity is acknowledged by his natural father, he may petition for a royal warrant by which the arms of his father are granted, together with an appropriate mark of distinction. Again subject to a royal licence, adopted children may now use the arms of their adoptive parents which they difference with a mark depicting two interlaced links of chain.

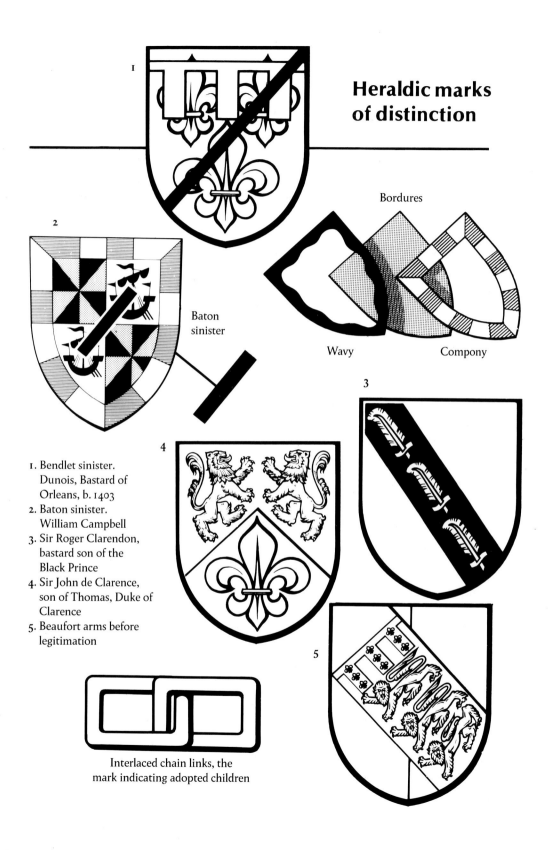

Heraldic marks of distinction

Bordures

Baton sinister

Wavy

Company

1. Bendlet sinister.
   Dunois, Bastard of
   Orleans, b. 1403
2. Baton sinister.
   William Campbell
3. Sir Roger Clarendon,
   bastard son of the
   Black Prince
4. Sir John de Clarence,
   son of Thomas, Duke of
   Clarence
5. Beaufort arms before
   legitimation

Interlaced chain links, the
mark indicating adopted children

Appendix 1   Further Reading

Dennys, R. *The Heraldic Imagination*, London, 1975
Friar, S. *A New Dictionary of Heraldry*, London, 1987
Friar, S. *Heraldry for the Local Historian and Genealogist*, Stroud, Glos., 1992
Woodcock, T. & Robinson, J. M. *The Oxford Guide to Heraldry*, Oxford, 1988

Appendix 2   Useful Addresses

American College of Heraldry, Drawer CG, University of Alabama, Tuscaloosa, AL 35486–2870, USA

British Information Services, 845 Third Avenue, New York, NY 10022–6691, USA

Chief Herald of Canada, The Canadian Heraldic Authority, Rideau Hall, Ottawa, Ontario, Canada K1A 0A1

Chief Herald of Ireland's Office, 2 Kildare Street, Dublin, Republic of Ireland

College of Arms, Queen Victoria Street, London, England EC4V 4BT

College of Arms Foundation Inc. USA, c/o The College of Arms

Flag Research Center, 3 Edgehill Road, Winchester, MA 01890, USA

Heraldry Group, Genealogical Society of Victoria, PO Box 1207, Bundoora, Victoria 3083, Australia

Heraldry Society, 44–45 Museum Street, London, England WC1A 1LY

Heraldry Society (New Zealand Branch), 60 Sayegn Street, St Heliers, Auckland, New Zealand

Heraldry Society of Canada, PO Box 8467, Station T, Ottawa, Ontario K1G 3H9, Canada

Heraldry Society of Ireland, Castle Matrix, Rathkeale, Co Limerick, Republic of Ireland

Heraldry Society of Scotland, 25 Craigentinny Crescent, Edinburgh EH7 6QA

Institute of Heraldic and Genealogical Studies, Northgate, Canterbury, Kent, England CT1 1BA

Lord Lyon King of Arms and the Court of Lord Lyon, H. M. New Register House, Edinburgh, Scotland EH1 3YT

New Zealand Herald of Arms Extraordinary, Executive Council Chambers, Parliament Buildings, Wellington, New Zealand

Society of Heraldic Arts, 46 Reigate Road, Reigate, Surrey RH2 0QN

Index

Heraldic terms, and non-English words, are shown in *italics*. Page numbers in *italics* refer to illustrations and those in **bold italics** to colour plate numbers.